Y0-BRW-771

TRANSPORTATION, DISTRIBUTION & LOGISTICS

Education

Bothell, WA • Chicago, IL • Columbus, OH • New York, NY

Image Credits: Cover Photo: F1 ONLINE/SuperStock.

www.mheonline.com

 **Education**

Send all inquiries to:
McGraw-Hill Education
130 East Randolph Street, Suite 400
Chicago, IL 60601

ISBN: 978-0-07-661079-2
MHID: 0-07-661079-9

Printed in the United States of America.

1 2 3 4 5 6 7 8 9 RHR 17 16 15 14 13 12 11

CAREER COMPANION
TRANSPORTATION, DISTRIBUTION, & LOGISTICS

CONTENTS

TO THE STUDENT

EXPLORING AND PREPARING FOR A CAREER IN TRANSPORTATION, DISTRIBUTION, AND LOGISTICS

This resource booklet is designed to introduce you to the transportation, distribution, and logistics industry. It will tell you about the variety of jobs in the industry and how to build a career in this field. It will also provide the opportunity to practice the skills that will help you succeed in the industry. Explore the transportation, distribution, and logistics industry and practice the skills presented to help you decide if this industry is right for you.

Finding a job that interests you is the first step in managing your career. To be successful, however, you'll need to explore many job and career possibilities. What if your goals change? What if there is a shift in the labor market or the economy? You may need, or want, to change jobs or even careers. By improving your transferable skills, such as speaking, writing, organizing, planning, and problem solving, you will make yourself a more valuable employee and be able to cope with changes in the labor market. The more transferable skills you develop, the greater your chance of success at any job.

When considering a career in the transportation, distribution, and logistics industry, it is important to understand the realities of the industry. Which jobs have the strongest growth? Which offer good opportunities for advancement? Which jobs align most closely with your own abilities and interests? Are there many jobs available in your area?

Keep these questions in mind as you read Part I of this Career Companion booklet. When you have finished, refer to them again and see how many you can answer. Do the answers make you more or less likely to want to work in this industry? If you feel this industry may be right for you, work your way through the practice questions in Part II. Using real-world situations, they will help you begin preparing for any career in the transportation, distribution, and logistics industry.

EXPLORE

This section of *Career Companion: Transportation, Distribution, and Logistics* will introduce you to the transportation, distribution, and logistics industry.

You will explore the following topics:

THE TRANSPORTATION, DISTRIBUTION, AND LOGISTICS INDUSTRY

TRANSPORTATION, DISTRIBUTION, AND LOGISTICS JOBS

BUILDING A CAREER IN TRANSPORTATION, DISTRIBUTION, AND LOGISTICS

EDUCATION AND TRAINING

WORKING IN THE TRANSPORTATION, DISTRIBUTION, AND LOGISTICS INDUSTRY

INDUSTRY TRENDS

CAREER RESOURCES

After exploring this industry, you will be able to answer the following questions:
- What kinds of jobs are available in this industry?
- How can I match my skills and interests with the right job?
- What are the training requirements for these jobs?
- What skills are needed to work in this field?
- What factors affect trends in the industry?

As you read this book, think about whether the careers described are right for you.

CHAPTER 1

THE TRANSPORTATION, DISTRIBUTION, AND LOGISTICS INDUSTRY

Did you take a bus to get somewhere today? Did you buy food at the supermarket? If you did, you used the services provided by workers in the transportation, distribution, and logistics industry.

What exactly are transportation, distribution, and logistics? These terms are closely related. **Transportation** is the movement of people, goods, and services from one place to another. **Distribution** is coordinating the shipment and delivery of goods and services. **Logistics** is planning the movement of people, goods, services, information, and money.

Goods being moved are known as freight or cargo. Millions of workers keep the transportation system moving along a wide network of roads, airports, railroads, and waterways. They operate or repair planes, trains, and other vehicles. They supervise airports, warehouses, and ship yards. Without them, everyday life could not function. Without them, the American economy would collapse.

Career Pathways in This Industry

A **career cluster** is a grouping of jobs and industries based on common characteristics. A **career pathway** is an area of focus within a career cluster. The transportation, distribution, and logistics career cluster has seven pathways:

- **Transportation Operations**
- **Logistics Planning and Management Services**
- **Warehousing and Distribution Center Operations**
- **Sales and Service**
- **Facility and Mobile Equipment Maintenance**
- **Health, Safety, and Environmental Management**
- **Transportation Systems/Infrastructure Planning, Management, and Regulation**

TRANSPORTATION OPERATIONS

The transportation operations pathway involves the operation and support of all transportation vehicles. It includes those who drive or help operate the vehicles, like truck drivers and flight attendants. It includes people who work behind the scenes, such as air traffic controllers and taxi dispatchers.

Workers in this career pathway may be employed by the government (public sector) or by a private company (private sector). They may transport passengers, freight, or both. Bus drivers carry passengers. Many bus drivers work for the public school system, transporting students to and from school. Other bus drivers operate the publicly owned buses used to transport commuting workers and other passengers around large cities or between cities and suburbs. Mass transit also employs workers who help operate passenger trains and subways.

Many operators of rail transportation carry freight for private railroad companies. Truck drivers usually work for private companies. These drivers include truckload (TL) carriers, who transport a shipment to its destination, and less-than-truckload (LTL) carriers, who combine small shipments from different customers to create a larger load.

Some airline pilots fly planes for the US military. But many pilots work in the private sector. They pilot passenger planes. They also pilot planes that carry freight, such as packages and express mail. Similarly, in water transportation, many captains, pilots, and mates work for the merchant marine or the navy. Others, however, help operate privately owned boats and ships. These include tugboats, cruise ships, and sightseeing boats.

LOGISTICS PLANNING AND MANAGEMENT SERVICES

The logistics planning and management services pathway involves planning, managing, and controlling the movement of people and freight. It includes issues such as strategy, budgeting, resource usage, facilities layout, inventory control, personnel, and scheduling.

Logistics analysts, engineers, and managers collect and analyze data related to the movement of people and freight. They then provide the most efficient solution for each transportation situation.

CAREER PATHWAYS AND OCCUPATION	PROJECTED JOB GROWTH 2008–2018
Transportation Operations	
Truck Drivers, Heavy and Tractor-Trailer	554,600
Truck Drivers, Light or Delivery Services	217,500
Industrial Truck and Tractor Operators	198,600
Bus Drivers, School	107,100
Taxi Drivers and Chauffeurs	77,300
Bus Drivers, Transit and Intercity	49,900
Locomotive Engineers	21,600
Railroad Conductors and Yardmasters	17,000
Logistics Planning and Management Services	
Logistics Managers	297,500
Logisticians	41,900
Warehousing and Distribution Center Operations	
Laborers and Freight Movers, Hand	745,800
Supply Chain Managers	297,500
Shipping, Receiving, and Traffic Clerks	186,200
Packers and Packagers, Hand	126,100
Freight Forwarders	40,300
Sales and Service	
Billing and Posting Clerks and Machine Operators	167,600
Cargo and Freight Agents	40,300
Facility and Mobile Equipment Maintenance	
Automotive Master Mechanics	181,700
Vehicle and Equipment Cleaners	127,700
Bus / Truck Mechanics and Diesel Engine Specialists	75,300
Automotive Body and Related Repairs	43,800
Health, Safety, and Environmental Management	
Industrial Safety and Health Engineers	9,200
Planning, Management, and Regulation	
Customs Brokers	368,300
Transportation Planners	23,800
Transportation Vehicle, Equipment and Systems Inspectors, except Avian	11,300

Source: O*Net Occupational Network Database

WAREHOUSING AND DISTRIBUTION CENTER OPERATIONS

Warehouses and distribution centers store goods until the goods are ready to be shipped to their destination. They store general merchandise and refrigerated goods. Some provide special atmospheres, where temperature, humidity, and gases in the air are carefully controlled to minimize food spoilage and extend storage times.

Jobs in this career pathway involve packaging, loading, and tracking goods that are ready for transport. Operations managers oversee the facilities. Material movers load and unload freight. Shipping, receiving, and traffic clerks make sure that orders are filled and that documents and records are correct.

SALES AND SERVICE

Jobs in the sales and service pathway involve marketing and selling transportation services for people or freight. Ticket and reservations agents, for example, make reservations and sell and exchange tickets for passenger travel. Travel agents help plan people's trips. Customer service representatives assist passengers and address the special needs that customers may have. Sales managers help sell the services of transportation companies, including companies that ship freight. Billing clerks send out bills and record payments. Marketing managers perform market research, identify potential markets, and create a company's marketing strategy.

FACILITY AND MOBILE EQUIPMENT MAINTENANCE

Those who work in the facility and mobile equipment maintenance pathway maintain and repair transportation vehicles and related equipment. They are also responsible for maintenance and repairs of warehouses and other facilities.

Many workers specialize in a particular type of repair. For example, some aircraft mechanics specialize in an airplane's electrical system. Railroad track workers specialize in maintaining and repairing tracks. Diesel mechanics repair buses and large trucks that run on diesel fuel. Automotive mechanics repair smaller trucks and other small motor vehicles. Service technicians make sure that vehicles and equipment are in working order.

HEALTH, SAFETY, AND ENVIRONMENTAL MANAGEMENT

Workers in the health, safety, and environmental management pathway identify and manage safety risks and possible environmental hazards. They address dangers to the health and safety of workers, passengers, and communities. Often they help develop company safety practices. They may also run training sessions to improve on-the-job safety and help workers avoid accidents.

Environmental protection specialists check that food, water, and air meet government standards. They suggest ways to stop or clean up pollution.

TRANSPORTATION SYSTEMS/INFRASTRUCTURE PLANNING, MANAGEMENT, AND REGULATION

The planning, management, and regulation pathway focuses on the planning and management of the public transportation infrastructure. This includes roads, bridges, rail lines, and all other transportation facilities needed for the operation of the economy. Many workers in this pathway are employed by federal, state, or local government transportation agencies. Those in the private sector often work for architectural and engineering firms.

Urban and regional planners look for the best ways to meet the transportation needs of communities. Civil engineers design and maintain parts of the transportation infrastructure. Government regulators and inspectors develop transportation safety rules and make sure those rules are followed.

Industry Outlook

The outlook for the transportation, distribution, and logistics industry is average overall. International and cross-country shipping will continue to increase. This will mean job growth in transportation as well as in warehousing and logistics. Increases in online ordering will also help increase jobs in trucking and warehousing. All these jobs, however, are linked to the health of the economy.

Opportunities for military jobs are expected to be excellent. Government jobs overall, however, are expected to decline due to decreasing budgets. Population growth and higher fuel costs will mean some growth in jobs for mass transit. Health, safety, the environment, and the decaying infrastructure all remain key public concerns. Both government and private sector jobs that address these concerns should continue to grow.

TRANSPORTATION, DISTRIBUTION, AND LOGISTICS JOB OUTLOOK BY CAREER PATHWAY 2008–2018

PATHWAY	JOB OUTLOOK
Transportation Operations	• Truck driving jobs should increase by about 11 percent. • The US military offers opportunities for airline pilots. Military training will also help in finding commercial jobs later. • Mass transit demands will mean more jobs for bus and rail operators. • Jobs operating boats and ships should see better than average growth due to tourism and offshore drilling. • Jobs operating ferries will increase in some cities. • Jobs for taxi drivers should show growth if the economy improves.
Logistics Planning and Management Services	• The increasingly global economy will mean a greater demand for logistics services. • Many jobs will be with third-party logistics providers. 3PL providers offer services to companies without their own logistics capabilities.
Warehousing and Distribution Center Operations	• Warehousing and distribution centers should see good job growth as more companies contract out their warehousing needs. • Material movers will have better opportunities in warehouses than in other worksites. • Clerk positions should increase along with other warehousing jobs.
Sales and Service	• Global competition will create a greater need for effective marketing. • College graduates with the right technical knowledge and people skills are likely to get the best sales jobs. • Opportunities for travel, reservation, and ticket agents will decline as more passengers use the Internet to plan trips and buy tickets.
Facility and Mobile Equipment Maintenance	• Jobs in facility maintenance will see below average growth as new computer programs diagnose problems for faster, easier repairs. • Growth in automotive and diesel mechanics jobs will be slow since more durable vehicles are being built. These will need fewer repairs.
Health, Safety, and Environmental Management	• Despite budget problems, public concerns will mean more government jobs in healthy and safety management. • Public concerns and new environmental laws will lead to a large increase in environmental management jobs. • Growth will be strongest for positions in environmental consulting firms in the private sector.
Planning, Management, and Regulation	• The decaying infrastructure will create demand for many professionals in this career pathway. • Civil engineering jobs are expected to grow by as much as 24 percent.

Source: US Department of Labor, *Career Guide to Industries 2010–11* and *Occupational Outlook Handbook 2010–11*

TRANSPORTATION, DISTRIBUTION, AND LOGISTICS JOBS

The transportation, distribution, and logistics industry offers a great variety of jobs. You can find jobs at all skill levels, from entry level to managerial. Do you want to make transportation more efficient? Would you like to fly an airplane? These job profiles will introduce you to some professions in the industry.

CAREER PATHWAY ▶ Transportation Operations

TRANSIT AND INTERCITY BUS DRIVER

Bus drivers pick up and drop off passengers at scheduled times and locations. Some drive buses that travel along a regular route. Others drive buses chartered for special trips. The main responsibilities of all bus drivers are driving safely and being on schedule. Often bus drivers collect fares, announce stops, and help elderly and disabled passengers. On intercity routes, bus drivers may move and stow baggage.

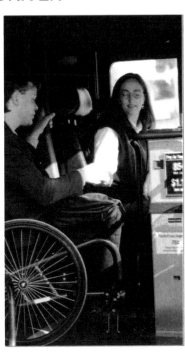

Special Skills Bus drivers must earn a commercial driver's license. Good bus drivers are patient and alert at all times. They must be able to handle large groups of people. They also need a good sense of direction and the ability to read maps.

RAILROAD CONDUCTOR

Railroad conductors are responsible for the safety of train passengers, cargo, and crews. They get instructions from dispatchers about the train's route, timetable, and cargo. During the run, they signal to the engineer when the train should stop, start, and change speeds. On passenger trains, they may collect tickets, make announcements, and help passengers board and depart. On freight trains, they make sure cars are added or removed at the right points. They report on arrival and departure times and on passengers or freight carried.

Special Skills Railroad conductors need good written and oral communication skills. They must know how to read route maps, passenger and cargo lists, and other documents. They must be familiar with train equipment, tracks, and signals. They must be able to identify mechanical problems and resolve emergencies quickly and safely. They need to work well with the public and with all levels of railroad personnel.

INDUSTRIAL TRUCK AND TRACTOR OPERATOR

Industrial truck and tractor operators use industrial trucks and tractors to move materials. They work in a variety of places, including factories, storage yards, construction sites, and warehouses. Some drive forklifts, a machine that moves and lifts heavy objects. Others use tractors to pull trailers filled with heavy materials and equipment.

Special Skills Industrial truck and tractor operators need to be good drivers and have good coordination. They should have steady hands and good depth perception. They should understand the gauges and dials of trucks and tractors to make sure the machines are working properly.

HEAVY TRUCK AND TRACTOR-TRAILER DRIVER

Heavy truck and tractor-trailer drivers, also known as over-the-road truck drivers, deliver goods in large trucks and tractor-trailers. Some travel on a set route or around one region of the United States. Others travel all over the country, and they may even go to Mexico or Canada. All these drivers are given a delivery location and a deadline, but they plan their own routes. They must keep logs showing that they have followed government rules for traveling in heavy trucks. In some cases, two drivers may travel together, with one sleeping while the other drives.

Special Skills Drivers should be responsible, self-motivated, and able to work with little supervision. Many companies require drivers to be at least 22 years old and able to lift heavy objects.

LIGHT OR DELIVERY SERVICE TRUCK DRIVER

Drivers of light trucks and delivery service vehicles deliver goods in a small region. They may take goods from a warehouse or distribution area and drop them off at a home or a business. Some load up their trucks once and spend the day making deliveries. Others return to the distribution center to make multiple pickups. Drivers sometimes accept payments and give bills or receipts to customers when they make their deliveries.

Special Skills Light truck drivers should have good social skills, since they spend a great deal of time dealing with people. They should have self-confidence, initiative, and tact. They may need to be able to handle heavy materials. They must be good drivers.

CAREER PATHWAY ▶ Logistics Planning and Management Services

LOGISTICS MANAGER

Logistics managers plan and direct the purchasing, warehousing, and distribution of goods. They determine the most efficient and cost-effective way of transporting goods and supplies. They create and use flow systems to meet production and distribution needs. They analyze the financial cost of logistics changes, such as new carriers or detours in the route. They also make sure companies follow all laws and regulations.

Special Skills Logistics managers must be good with details and organized. They require strong writing and speaking skills. They also need solid math, computer, and financial skills. They must be good at negotiating and problem solving, especially on tight deadlines. They need to be good leaders and team players. They must keep up with regulations and infrastructure changes.

CAREER PATHWAY ▶ Warehousing and Distribution Center Operations

FREIGHT, STOCK, AND MATERIAL MOVER

Freight, stock, and material movers move cargo on and off vehicles, ships, dock, or containers. They move items in and out of warehouses. The cargo is usually in heavy crates, boxes, and drums. To move the cargo, they use industrial trucks and tractors or ship loading and unloading equipment. They may use small vehicles with movable platforms called forklifts. While their main duty is moving materials, they may also make minor repairs to their equipment.

Special Skills Freight, stock, and material movers must be skilled in operating their vehicles. Physical fitness, good coordination, and good depth perception are important traits. They need to ensure the safety of others and of their equipment. They require good mechanical skills so they can maintain and repair their equipment.

FREIGHT FORWARDER

Freight forwarders arrange for the shipping of products. They research and select the most cost-effective and efficient shipping routes. They decide on the best modes of transportation to use. They may decide to group together goods from different shipments to save on costs. They reserve space for their shipments and prepare shipping documents. Once shipping is completed, they arrange for the delivery or storage of the goods.

Special Skills Freight forwarders must be familiar with all modes of transportation. They must be organized and have good math and computer skills. They must know how to read and fill out complicated documents.

 ## Sales and Service

BILLING AND POSTING CLERK AND MACHINE OPERATOR

Billing and posting clerks and machine operators prepare bills for shipping, warehousing, and other services. They gather the data needed for billing. They resolve mismatching information. They use computer software and office machinery to calculate and generate invoices. They send the bills to customers.

Special Skills Billing and posting clerks require strong computer and math skills. They have to keep up with the changing technology they may need to use. They must be organized and good with details. They also must be able to listen to and understand information presented by others.

CARGO AND FREIGHT AGENT

Cargo and freight agents arrange the shipping of freight at air, train, and trucking terminals and at shipping docks. They take orders from customers and provide information on payment methods. They prepare bills of lading (which confirm that shipments have been received), invoices, and other shipping documents. They arrange for the pickup and delivery of goods. They trace lost items.

Special Skills Cargo and freight agents need to be good at solving problems. They must be organized and careful with details. They need good speaking and listening skills. They must understand complex written instructions. They need math skills to understand pricing and scheduling.

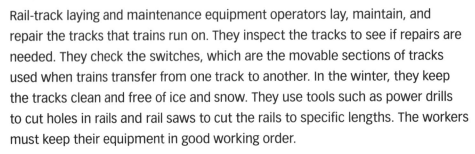

CAREER PATHWAY ▶ Facility and Mobile Equipment Maintenance

RAIL-TRACK LAYING AND MAINTENANCE EQUIPMENT OPERATOR

Rail-track laying and maintenance equipment operators lay, maintain, and repair the tracks that trains run on. They inspect the tracks to see if repairs are needed. They check the switches, which are the movable sections of tracks used when trains transfer from one track to another. In the winter, they keep the tracks clean and free of ice and snow. They use tools such as power drills to cut holes in rails and rail saws to cut the rails to specific lengths. The workers must keep their equipment in good working order.

Special Skills Rail-track laying and maintenance equipment operators require a strong knowledge of machinery and construction. They need sound judgment in determining when things are wrong or about to go wrong. They must have steady arms and hands, good coordination, and a sharp eye for detail. They need to be patient and precise, since they often must perform the same task many times to get it exactly right. They must be careful to ensure their own safety and the safety of others.

AUTOMOTIVE MASTER MECHANIC

Automotive master mechanics repair cars, trucks, and other motor vehicles. They also do routine maintenance on motor vehicles. Some mechanics work on many parts of the vehicle. Others specialize in a particular part, such as the transmission. They examine and test-drive the vehicle to learn what is wrong and discuss the problem with the vehicle operator or owner. They then make the necessary repairs, using checklists to make sure they look at every problem spot. When a job is completed, they make sure the vehicle operator or owner knows anything necessary to avoid experiencing problems while operating the vehicle.

Special Skills Automotive master mechanics need a strong knowledge of machinery, tools, and motor vehicles. They must be able to identify problems and find solutions. They must be active listeners and good at explaining problems and solutions to those who seek their help. They need steady hands and good coordination. They must have good vision so they can examine small parts. They also need a strong sense of hearing, since some mechanical problems are heard, not seen.

CAREER PATHWAY ▶ Health, Safety, and Environmental Management

INDUSTRIAL SAFETY AND HEALTH ENGINEER

Industrial safety and health engineers plan and manage programs to prevent unsafe work conditions. They look for safety problems by inspecting work sites and interviewing employees. When an accident occurs, they study the cause of the accident and then find ways to correct problems. They make sure new safety devices are installed on equipment and at work sites.

Special Skills Industrial safety and health engineers must have an in-depth understanding of how equipment works. They must be familiar with safety regulations. They must be effective communicators who are able to motivate others to use safe practices on the work site.

CAREER PATHWAY ▶ Planning, Management, and Regulation

TRANSPORTATION PLANNER

Transportation planners study proposed transportation projects and make recommendations about the projects. They evaluate needs and analyze costs. They work closely with engineers to resolve problems. Transportation planners conduct surveys and hold public hearings to get input about proposed projects.

Special Skills Transportation planners need a strong background in engineering. They should have good math and computer skills. Strong speaking and writing skills are also important. Finally, they must be able to put together information from many sources and draw conclusions based on that information.

CUSTOMS BROKER

Customs brokers make sure shipments meet all regulations for import (receiving) and export (sending out). They prepare shipping documents. They calculate taxes and fees. They represent their clients at meetings with customs officials.

Special Skills Customs brokers must obtain licenses from the US government to show that they are familiar with import/export regulations, taxes, and fees. Customs brokers need strong reading and math skills so they can understand complex documents and calculate taxes and fees. They must be well organized, and they must have good communication and problem-solving skills.

BUILDING A CAREER IN TRANSPORTATION, DISTRIBUTION, AND LOGISTICS

Once you have chosen a field that interests you, look ahead and consider your career path. This path is made up of the job experiences and career moves that lead you toward your career goal. You may take several steps before reaching your ultimate goal. You will likely spend time in an entry-level position. This will help you gain the professional experience needed to move ahead in your career.

For example, a worker that wants to be a supervisor of a material and distribution operation might begin in an entry-level position as a manual laborer in the distribution center. More experience may lead to a mid-level position as a machine operator. The next step may be an advanced job repairing and maintaining the equipment, and that might lead to a promotion as an assistant supervisor in charge of maintenance and repair. Finally, the worker could be promoted to supervisor of the entire distribution operation.

Don't worry if you change your mind about your career path. This happens to many people. It often takes time to find the right path. You can always change your career path regardless of where you are in your chosen profession.

Evaluating Career Choices

Choosing a career is challenging. Now is a good time to start thinking about what kind of career path you would like to follow. A well-chosen career can bring satisfaction and success in life.

Self-knowledge is the key to making wise career choices. Friends, teachers, and family members may offer helpful suggestions for potential careers. However, you are ultimately in charge of making your own career decisions.

Consider your personality, interests, aptitudes, and values when choosing a career. Think about why you chose to read this book. Of the many industries in which you could work, why does this industry appeal to you?

You might feel that your personality, the way you think and behave, is well suited to this industry. If you are a practical, independent person who likes solving problems and helping others, then a career in this field may be a good choice.

You should also consider your interests when making career decisions. What activities do you enjoy? Do you like working with computers or planning trips? What classes did you like most in high school? People who enjoy transportation, distribution, and logistics are usually interested in math, business, or travel.

In some cases, your aptitude, or ability in a certain area, will shape your career goals. Ask yourself what skills come naturally to you. A strong aptitude in math may help you succeed as a logistics manager or a billing clerk. However, aptitude is not the same as interest. You may have strong mechanical abilities, for example, but you might prefer a career that uses other skills.

Values are another factor to consider when selecting a career. Values are the principles and beliefs that you live by. You might value responsibility, compassion, independence, and creativity. Your values will shape all areas of your life, from your long-term goals to the lifestyle you lead. For example, if being a responsible family member is important to you, you might seek a job that allows for flextime and provides good vacation benefits.

Success in the Transportation, Distribution, and Logistics Career Cluster

As you have learned, the career opportunities in the transportation, distribution, and logistics industry are broad enough to accommodate workers with a variety of personality traits, interests, aptitudes, and values.

Your satisfaction with working in the transportation, distribution, and logistics industry will depend on how well you match yourself to a particular job. If you are uncertain about your desired career path, there are resources that can help you. You can take self-assessment tests to find a career that matches your strengths. Part-time or temporary work can also help you discover your aptitudes and interests.

The careers profiled in this book represent just some of the types of jobs available in this industry. There are too many jobs to list in just one book. The workplace is constantly changing. Opportunities in traditional fields continue to expand, and new opportunities are constantly arising.

Learning about the range of job opportunities available to you will give you an advantage when you begin your job search. Developing workplace skills and learning about all aspects of the architecture and construction industry will also help you. As you make your career choices, think positively, keeping in mind your best attributes. Set ambitious but realistic goals, and keep an open mind about opportunities that may arise.

Working with Data, People, and Things

Most careers offer opportunities to work with a combination of data, people, and things. Working with data involves the evaluation of information. Working with people requires building human relationships. Working with things involves using tools, objects, and machines. Most jobs focus mainly on one of these. Billing clerks, for example, work mainly with data. Flight attendants work primarily with people. Mechanics work mostly with things. When planning your career path, consider what balance of data, people, and things you want.

CAREERS THAT INVOLVE WORKING WITH DATA

Working with data means working with words, ideas, concepts, and numbers. Examples of working with data include compiling packing lists, preparing budgets, and scheduling the steps required to move a product from manufacturer to consumer. These tasks require good math, verbal, and organizational skills. The tasks often involve using computers.

A number of jobs in the transportation, distribution, and logistics industry focus on working with data. Cargo and freight agents, for example, record orders, provide payment methods, and prepare documents that list data about shipments. Billing clerks compile and list services performed and the costs of those services. Transportation planners collect and analyze data to make decisions about the design of highways, airports, and bus systems.

As an airline dispatcher, you might keep track of flight data for as many as 12 planes at a time. You need to track each plane's route, speed, and changes in altitude; keep records of the weight of the plane's cargo and amount of fuel; and know the amount of time by each member of the crew has flown. In addition, you need to keep track of landing plans and weather conditions.

Are you good with words and numbers? Do you enjoy applying scientific and mathematical principles to everyday situations? Do you grasp new concepts quickly? Do people say that you think logically? If so, you may want to consider a career that focuses on working with data.

CAREERS THAT INVOLVE WORKING WITH PEOPLE

Working with people refers to jobs dealing mainly with human relationships. Examples of working with people include serving passengers, training or supervising employees, and advising customers. All these activities require strong communications skills.

Quite a few jobs in transportation, distribution, and logistics focus on working with people. They include many jobs in passenger transportation. Taxi and bus drivers, railroad conductors on passenger trains, flight attendants, and reservations and ticket agents work with passengers for most of the day. They often interact during busy travel times, when passengers' tempers may be short.

Other transportation, distribution, and logistics jobs require working with coworkers in teams. Managers or supervisors must effectively lead teams of workers. Workers in teams must be able to follow directions and communicate ideas to one another.

People who enjoy working with other people are generally outgoing. To decide if you're a "people person," ask yourself a few questions. Do you place great emphasis on your friendships with others? Do you spend your spare time socializing with friends or family? Are you good at judging the motivations and feelings of others? If so, you'll probably enjoy a job that allows for frequent interaction with others.

CAREERS THAT INVOLVE WORKING WITH THINGS

Working with things refers to jobs dealing with goods, machinery, tools, and other objects. Examples of working with things include operating vehicles, loading freight, and repairing equipment. All of these activities require strong mechanical skills.

Many careers in transportation, distribution, and logistics involve working mainly with things. Diesel, automotive, boat, and airline mechanics spend most of their days working with tools, parts, and electronic testing equipment. Rail-track layers use tools and equipment to lay, maintain, and repair the tracks that trains run on. Material movers at docks, warehouses, and distribution centers use special vehicles and other equipment to load and unload freight.

Think about how you choose to spend your spare time. Do you enjoy building, assembling, or repairing things? Are you curious about how machines like cars or computers actually work? Do you prefer to work with your hands? If so, you're probably well suited for working with things.

DATA, PEOPLE, AND THINGS IN THE TRANSPORTATION, DISTRIBUTION, AND LOGISTICS INDUSTRY

Whatever career in transportation, distribution, and logistics you choose, you are likely to spend some time working with data, people, and things. Choosing a job that matches what you like to do will make you a better employee and a happier person.

How can you find a job that best suits your strengths? One way is by browsing the Dictionary of Occupational Titles (www.occupationalinfo.org). This resource lists a wide range of jobs. Each job has a nine-digit code that identifies and describes it. The fourth, fifth, and sixth digits show how much each job involves working with data, people, and things, respectively. The lower the number, the more complex the particular type of work. For example, a logistics manager's DOT code is 019.167-010. The numbers 1,6, and 7 mean that the job involves complex work with data, much simpler work with people, and even simpler work with things.

Finding Employment

Finding a job is seldom easy, but finding a job in a new career field can be especially hard. Whether you have a job but are considering a career change or you are unemployed, now is a good time to explore new careers and make yourself more interesting to employers.

CHANGING CAREERS

Many people jump from one career right into another. They may feel that their job does not match their skills or interests. They may believe the job does not offer enough room to advance. A new career can offer different opportunities.

The best time to think about a new career is when you are already employed. While you have a job, there is less pressure to find a new job right away. Investigate which career fields have good opportunities in the area where you live. Think about your current job. What aspects of the job do you enjoy? Which other careers that involve similar tasks?

If you find a job that you would like to pursue, spend time investigating the qualifications required. You might speak to someone who works in the industry. Learn as much as you can to ensure the career cluster is right for you.

Look for ways you can gain experience that will help you in your search. If the new career involves working with people, volunteer for tasks in which you will interact with people.

You should spend time creating a résumé. Use print and online resources to learn how to create the résumé that best highlights your qualifications. Highlight the skills that are most relevant to the jobs you will apply for.

You should also spend time networking, or reaching out to people who can help in your job search. This may include family, friends, or colleagues from current or former jobs. Make an effort to meet new people to expand your network. One good way to do this is to use online networking sites.

UNEMPLOYMENT

Being unemployed can be a difficult time, but it can bring new opportunities. Millions of people are unemployed at any time, so there is no shame in being unemployed. If you are unemployed, apply for unemployment benefits. Benefits are given only after you are approved, so be sure to apply right away.

Make the most of the time you are unemployed. Work on your résumé. Expand your network. Try to stick to a daily schedule. For example, you might shower and dress as if going to work and then spend the morning crafting your résumé or searching for jobs. Rather than spending every waking hour looking for work, set aside some time for leisure activities.

Consider finding a freelance or part-time job that can help you gain new skills and earn more money while you search. You might also take a class that teaches skills useful in a new career.

EDUCATION AND TRAINING

Jobs in the transportation, distribution, and logistics industry require varying levels of education. Many jobs in this industry require little or no formal training. For others, it is necessary to have specific education and experience.

Training and Education for Transportation, Distribution, and Logistics

The level of training necessary to succeed in the transportation, distribution, and logistics industry varies by career. Jobs can be categorized into three groups— those requiring little or no training, those requiring some training, and those requiring advanced training.

JOBS REQUIRING LITTLE OR NO TRAINING

Many jobs in this career cluster require little or no education or pre-employment training. Dock and marina workers and material movers at distribution centers, can often begin work without training. They usually get informal training on the job. Workers such as ticket and reservations agents may have workplace training program after they are hired.

However, getting a high school education or the equivalent is important. Many employers look for workers who earned solid grades in high school. Failing to complete high school may hurt your chances for advancement.

JOBS REQUIRING SOME TRAINING

Many jobs in transportation, distribution, and logistics require some training. Technical schools and community or junior colleges offer programs that can prepare you for jobs that demand specialized training, such as auto mechanics.

Training may also be obtained through trade organizations, such as the Professional Truck Driver Institute (PTDI). Such groups offer certification programs that provide training for a specific occupation. The program may require a minimum number of hours on the job and a minimum score on a test.

Earning an associate's degree or certification can help you get a job and advance in your field. For more information about such programs, contact community colleges, technical schools, and trade organizations in your area. You can also learn more about trade organizations by visiting the websites listed on page 38.

JOBS REQUIRING ADVANCED TRAINING

Some jobs in transportation, distribution, and logistics require more extensive training or formal education. To become a manager, you usually need at least a bachelor's degree from a four-year college. Experience may substitute for lack of higher education, but most managers have college degrees in business administration, organizational management, or marketing.

Many of the fastest-growing careers in this industry require college degrees. Logistics managers, for instance, are usually required to have at least a bachelor's degree in logistics or business management. Industrial safety and health engineers and environmental managers need advanced degrees. Professionals who manage the public transportation infrastructure often have a master's and even a doctoral degree.

TRAINING REQUIRED FOR TRANSPORTATION, DISTRIBUTION, AND LOGISTICS JOBS

Jobs Requiring Little or No Training

Automotive Body Repairers	Industrial Truck and Tractor Operators
Bus and Taxi Drivers	Railroad Signal and Switch Operators
Cargo and Freight Agents	Railroad Conductors and Yardmasters
Flight Attendants	Shipping, Receiving, and Traffic Clerks

Jobs Requiring Some Training or Education

Air Traffic Controllers	Avionics Technicians
Aircraft Mechanics Airfield	Material Movers
Automotive Master Mechanics	Ship and Boat Captains
Automotive Specialty Technicians	Ship Engineers

Jobs Requiring Advanced Training or Education

Airline Pilots and Flight Engineers	Storage and Distribution Managers
Freight and Cargo Inspectors	Supply Chain Managers
Industrial Safety Engineers	Transportation Managers

Certain jobs require a great deal of experience in addition to college degrees. Airline pilots, for instance, must have a minimum of 1,500 hours of flying time before they can captain a passenger plane. Deck officers on merchant vessels must accumulate thousands of hours of experience at sea.

Pre-Employment Training

Pre-employment training for jobs in transportation, distribution, and logistics may involve completing one or more of the following:

- an apprenticeship or internship

- a certification or specialized program at a technical school

- a bachelor's, master's, or doctoral degree program at a college or university

Before seeking formal training, look for ways to get on-the-job training. Many employers in this industry provide training for entry-level employees.

APPRENTICESHIPS

An apprenticeship is a way to gain work experience. In an apprenticeship, an inexperienced worker learns a trade by working alongside an expert worker. Some apprenticeships last as long as four or five years. Although apprentices earn little during that period, workers who complete apprenticeship programs are often well respected and well paid. Apprenticeships are available for careers such as able seamen and locomotive engineers. Unions and professional associations sometimes offer apprenticeships. The US Department of Labor's Office of Apprenticeship (http://oa.doleta.gov) is a good source of information.

INTERNSHIPS

An internship provides supervised practical experience. Internships are usually shorter than apprenticeships. They may offer the opportunity to learn about various jobs in a company. An intern often receives little or no pay, but completing an internship can improve your chances of getting a job.

TECHNICAL AND CAREER SCHOOLS

If you're interested in a position that requires some training, a technical school is a promising option. Technical school offers a variety of skills-oriented programs for trades such as automotive repair or avionics, the electronic systems on aircraft. They may also offer business programs such as operations management and international business.

Career schools specialize in training for one particular career or group of related careers. They may specialize in business, computer technology, or environmental health. Career schools that meet state requirements receive special licenses to operate. Some career schools, such as flight schools and maritime academies, are regulated by agencies of the federal government.

POSTSECONDARY EDUCATION

Most skilled and professional workers in the transportation, distribution, and logistics industry have completed at least some postsecondary education (study conducted after high school). Most people seek postsecondary education at universities, technical schools, or community colleges. Managers often have degrees in business, sometimes focusing on special areas such as logistics or organizational management. Other skilled workers may focus on technology or engineering.

To address the needs of busy professionals, many schools now offer online programs of postsecondary study. Often these programs focus on one particular subject area. These programs may offer certificates rather than degrees. These online programs can be especially helpful to someone already working who wants to change careers.

Before choosing a postsecondary educational program, think about several factors. Consider the length of the program and its rate of job placement. Find out whether the program is nationally accredited or state licensed. Take into account the school's reputation in the field and the expertise of its faculty. If you are currently working, consider whether you can fit the program into your daily schedule.

Another important factor is cost. You may be able to finance your education through loans, grants, work-study programs, or scholarships. Contact the financial aid office of the schools that interest you to find out which scholarships you might qualify for.

POSTGRADUATE EDUCATION

Postgraduate education is conducted after the completion of a bachelor's degree. Most people who seek postgraduate education enroll in a master's or doctoral degree program. In the transportation, distribution, and logistics industry, many logistics managers, government regulators, and environmental specialists have advanced degrees. Transportation, urban, and regional planners and civil engineers usually have advanced degrees as well. As competition for these jobs increases, having a master's or doctoral degree may give you an advantage when you apply for a job.

Some professionals put off graduate school. Instead, they take a lower-level job in their field after obtaining a bachelor's degree. Such a job allows them to gain experience and perhaps qualify for company-sponsored programs to pay for graduate school.

When admitting students to graduate school, universities consider candidates' academic records and their work experience. In most cases, admission is quite selective. Those who wish to earn postgraduate degrees must have strong academic backgrounds.

In recent years, some universities have begun offering postgraduate certificates as an alternative to degrees. Postgraduate certificate programs cost less and take less time than graduate school. These may be available online.

On-the-Job Training

On-the-job training is on-site instruction in how to perform a particular job. If you are seeking a position that requires little training, your employer will most likely train you.

On-the-job training has several benefits. One benefit is that you are usually paid while you are in training. However, even if you are not paid, you will be gaining knowledge and skill without paying tuition. Another benefit is that the training is tailored to the job. By the time you complete your training, you'll probably feel comfortable doing the work.

TYPES OF ON-THE-JOB TRAINING

Some on-the-job training is given individually to new employees. In other cases, small groups of employees who begin their jobs at about the same time are trained together. Some training is hands-on. It is given right in the workplace, with the new employee learning to drive a vehicle, repair equipment, or prepare invoices. Other training takes place in a classroom setting, with an instructor teaching or reinforcing skills.

Often classroom training combines with hands-on experience. New bus drivers, for example, usually spend time in a classroom learning safe driving practices and the special rules they need to know. They also spend time behind the wheel, learning how to operate a bus. With an experienced driver accompanying them, they make trial runs, picking up passengers and learning the route.

Many paid apprenticeships qualify as on-the-job training, especially if they are sponsored by the company employing the apprentice. Such programs may require the apprentice to work at the sponsor company for a certain length of time after complete the apprenticeship.

On-the-job training is available in many transportation, distribution, and logistics jobs. For instance, diesel mechanics, over-the-road truck drivers, and bridge and lock tenders often receive on-the-job training. Water transportation jobs have a long tradition of on-the-job training. Workers who start out as ordinary seamen or deckhands, for example, rise with training to the classification of able seamen. Ship pilots often go through a long period of apprenticeship with a towing company or harbor pilot's association.

On-the-job training is especially common for jobs in which workers are in high demand. As railway systems become more high-tech, for example, there is an increased need for workers who can operate and repair the new, more complex electronic equipment. When the supply of trained workers does not keep pace with the demand, many employers begin to provide more on-the-job training.

Job and Workplace Skills

When considering job candidates, employers look for both job-specific skills and general workplace skills. Job-specific skills are the skills necessary to do a particular job. For example, operating a forklift or completing a bill of lading is a job-specific skill. General workplace skills are skills that can be used in a variety of jobs.

TRANSPORTATION, DISTRIBUTION, AND LOGISTICS SKILL STANDARDS

Skills standards in the transportation, distribution, and logistics industry vary depending on the occupation. Many states have their own skill standards for some jobs. Federal agencies and nonprofit groups also maintain skill standards.

Skill standards for pilots, for example, are set by the Federal Aviation Administration (FAA). The FAA requires that all pilots pass a series of practical tests. They must demonstrate their ability to prepare for flight, to fly and maneuver, and to handle emergencies.

Skill standards for the merchant marine are set by the US Coast Guard. Specific standards govern all merchant-vessel jobs, such as able seaman and marine radio operator. Able seamen, for example, must have a certain number of days at sea and basic safety training. They also must pass either a coast guard exam or a coast guard-approved course.

Some nonprofit organizations focus on providing standards for training programs. These standards play a key role in turning out top-quality workers. For example, the National Automotive Technicians Education Foundation (NATEF) maintains standards for automotive mechanic training programs. These standards ensure that students who complete programs certified by NATEF have the skills to perform tasks expected of an automotive mechanic.

CORE SKILLS

Core skills differ from academic or job-specific skills. They are learned both inside and outside the classroom. They are also transferable from job to job. Developing these skills will make you more marketable in the transportation, distribution, and logistics industry, and in any job situation.

Communications Skills Communication skills are very important in the transportation, distribution, and logistics industry. Safety, on-time deliveries, and business success all depend on the ability to communicate clearly with customers and coworkers.

Listening Skills Listening skills are key to following instructions safely and precisely. They are vital to understanding what customers want. Good listening skills are also important in understanding the ideas and viewpoints of others.

Problem-Solving Skills Problem solving is essential to many jobs in transportation, distribution, and logistics. For example, a railroad conductor inspecting a train before a trip may be called on to troubleshoot problems related to defective cars. A logistics manager may need to deal with unexpected delays caused by a flood or a blizzard.

Technology Skills Modes of transportation, as well as distribution and logistics systems, involve increasingly complex technology. Workers must be able to keep up with these cutting-edge advances. In addition, many industry jobs require computer skills. Billing clerks, for example, use computer software to prepare invoices. Logistics managers use computers to prepare flow charts that help in planning the flow of goods.

Decision-Making Skills Being able to gather and analyze information quickly and to think clearly under pressure are skills required in many jobs in the transportation, distribution, and logistics industry. Railroad engineers, ship captains, and other transportation operators often face problems that require them to make quick decisions.

Organizing and Planning Skills Since efficient transportation involves so many steps, organization and planning are crucial. Planning requires setting goals and mapping out the steps leading needed to achieve these goals. This is the main function of logistics. It is also a central function of jobs such as freight forwarding and transportation management.

Teamwork Skills Teamwork is key to getting passengers or freight from point to point, especially if a variety of transportation methods is used. A complex vehicle or a vessel such as a plane, train, or ship can function only when every crew member works toward a common goal.

Social Skills Studies show that 80 to 85 percent of a person's success in the world of work is due to his or her social skills. Social interaction is basic to the customer service that must be provided in jobs dealing directly with clients or passengers. Social interaction with coworkers also makes for a better work atmosphere and happier workers.

Adaptability Skills Job descriptions, work environments, and work processes are constantly changing. New technology, economic changes, and changing customer tastes can require workers to adapt to new materials, techniques, and styles. Being able to acquire new skills and being ready to change increase your employability.

CHAPTER 5

WORKING IN THE TRANSPORTATION, DISTRIBUTION, AND LOGISTICS INDUSTRY

When choosing a career path, it is important to know what it is like to work in the industry. Understanding the work environment, hazards, and benefits of a job can help you make informed decisions.

Work Environment

Work environment refers to factors that affect workers' health and satisfaction on the job. These include the physical surroundings and the working hours. They also include the physical activities required to perform the job.

PHYSICAL ENVIRONMENT

People in the transportation, distribution, and logistics industry work in a variety of settings. Some are employed in comfortable offices. Others spend long periods of time in small spaces, noisy areas, or wet places. Material movers in ship and rail yards are outdoors in all weather conditions. Truck and bus drivers must drive in bad weather or heavy traffic. Ship pilots and able seamen often must work in damp and cold conditions.

Workplace conditions have improved because of new work-place laws. Modern equipment, safety precautions, and exhaust systems have also cut down on the dangerous and unpleasant conditions that were once more common in the industry.

WORK HOURS

Many employees in the transportation, logistics, and distribution industry work irregular hours. Ships, trains, buses, and other means of transportation often operate day and night, so employees must work in shifts. Shift work divides the day into blocks of time. Some workers start their shifts early in the morning. Others work night shifts. Many workers do not have weekends or holidays off.

The US Department of Transportation regulates the maximum number of hours that many industry employees can work. Generally speaking, transportation operators may work any time of day, but for safety reasons they cannot work overtime. Workers in warehouses and distribution centers, however, often work overtime to meet delivery demands. In the delivery business, late deliveries mean disappointed clients and lost business.

ESSENTIAL PHYSICAL ACTIVITIES

Work in the transportation, distribution, and logistics industry can be very physically demanding. Many workers perform heavy lifting or handle heavy equipment. Others drive or travel long hours under sometimes grueling conditions. Workers making repairs may need to crawl into confined spaces in or under vehicles.

Hazards and Environmental Dangers

According to the US Bureau of Labor Statistics, transportation and warehouse workers have a high risk of injury at work. The leading cause of on-the-job injuries is motor vehicle accidents. In fact, deaths from highway incidents were the most frequent kind of job-related fatality in 2009. Though air accidents were far less common, fatality figures were high when viewed as a percentage of the number of working pilots.

RATES OF WORK-RELATED INJURIES AND ILLNESSES IN THE TRANSPORTATION, DISTRIBUTION, AND LOGISTICS INDUSTRY PER 100 FULL-TIME WORKERS (2009)	
Occupation	Rate
Air transportation	8.5
Couriers and messengers	7.2
Warehousing and storage	5.9
Transportation and warehousing	5.2
Transit and ground passenger transportation	5.0
Truck transportation	4.6
Trade, transportation, and utilities	4.1
Support activities for transportation	4.0
Water transportation	2.5
Rail transportation	2.2
Pipeline transportation	1.9

Source: US Department of Labor

In warehouses and distribution centers, serious injuries often occur when equipment like forklifts tip over or strike or crush workers. Other common injuries include muscle strain from lifting heavy objects and bruises and broken bones from tripping and falling.

In addition to on-the-job-injuries, transportation workers risk chronic health dangers. Irregular schedules and frequent travel may cause exhaustion from lack of sleep. Airline personnel often experience jet lag, fatigue caused by traveling across several time zones. Those who work near engines and other noisy equipment face the danger of hearing loss.

WORKING CONDITIONS IN TRANSPORTATION, DISTRIBUTION, AND LOGISTICS

PATHWAY	CONDITIONS
Transportation Operations	• Many workers have irregular schedules, often working nights, weekends, and holidays. • Airline pilots, ship operators, and others who travel long distances are away from home for extended periods of time. • Some railroad workers sleep on board the trains they work on. Sleeping spaces are compact. They are usually more comfortable on passenger trains than freight trains. • Some long-distance trucks have sleeper cabs, refrigerators, and televisions. • Ship workers usually sleep on board in fairly comfortable quarters. • Vehicles and vessels must be driven or piloted in all kinds of weather conditions. • Bus, taxi, and truck drivers often drive in heavy traffic. • Truck drivers, airline pilots, and railroad engineers work in confined spaces. • Ship workers work in confined spaces that are often cold and damp. • Flight attendants and railroad conductors are often on their feet. • Truck drivers and ship workers may need to move heavy cargo. • Workers in passenger transportation may need to lift heavy luggage. • Ship workers must climb ladders from deck to deck. • Some workers on mass transit often climb up and down stairs. • Freight train operators may receive assignments on short notice. • Transit drivers who work alone sometimes face risks from dangerous passengers. • Taxi drivers risk robbery because they carry large amounts of cash and work alone.

PATHWAY	CONDITIONS
Logistics Planning and Management Services	• Logistics managers and analysts usually work in comfortable offices, but they may need to go on-site to address a problem. • Logistics managers often work overtime to meet tight deadlines.
Warehousing and Distribution Center Operations	• Material movers use vehicles that are hard to operate, so they risk accidents. • Heavy lifting and physical labor are often required. • Managers usually have offices, but they still spend time on the work floor. • Some cargo loaders work outside in all weather conditions. • Managers and workers often must work overtime to meet tight deadlines.
Sales and Service	• Many workers in sales and services work primarily on phones or computers during regular business hours. • Offices are usually comfortable, but individual work cubicles may be small. • Sales managers often travel to meet with clients and potential clients. • Marketing personnel spend time in the field to conduct surveys and other research. • Ticket agents at stations or terminals work in small areas and may stand for long periods of time.
Facility and Mobile Equipment Maintenance	• Workers often stand or lie in awkward positions while repairing equipment. • Oils, grease, and grime are generally present in the workplace. • Large garages usually provide comfortable work environments. • Smaller garages may have poor lighting, heating, and ventilation.
Health, Safety, and Environmental Management	• Health, safety, and environmental managers spend a great deal of time in the field monitoring conditions. • Health, safety, and environmental managers may work in offices when analyzing information and developing plans.
Planning, Management, and Regulation	• Transportation planners spend time in the field analyzing traffic and other conditions. • Regulators spend time in the field making inspections. • Transportation planners and regulators spend time in offices when developing plans and preparing reports.

SOURCE: US Department of Labor, *Career Guide to Industries 2010–11* and O*NET

Job Benefits

Benefits aren't just extras. They not only make your life easier and safer, but they be worth 20 to 35 percent of your salary.

Standard job benefits usually include paid health insurance, holidays, sick time, and vacations. At most companies, new employees do not start receiving paid vacation time until they have been on the job for 90 days or more. The specific job benefits you receive will depend on several factors, such as the size of organization you work for and the number of years you have been on the job.

At some companies, job benefits have expanded in recent years to include more than health insurance, paid vacation, and holidays, and sick leave. Some expanded benefits include the following:

- dental, life, and disability insurance

- time off to care for sick children

- tuition assistance

- 401(k) plan, or a retirement plan in which employees invest a portion of their income while employers match the contribution

- child-care assistance

Many transportation workers also get industry-specific benefits, known as perks. Airline employees and their partners, children, and parents may get free or discounted air travel when they go on vacation. They also may qualify for discounts at hotels and car rental agencies.

Labor Unions

A union is a group of workers who unite to bargain for job improvements.Union leaders negotiate with company management for better wages, increased benefits, better working conditions, and other job improvements. If an agreement is not reached, the union may use its most powerful tool—a strike. A strike occurs when employees stop working in an effort to force an employer to agree to the union's terms. In most cases, unions maintain strike funds, which provide partial salaries to striking workers.

When an agreement is reached between the union and company management, the company signs a labor contract. A labor contract is a legal agreement specifying wages, work hours, working conditions, and benefits. The union members must approve the contract before it goes into effect.

UNIONS IN TRANSPORTATION, DISTRIBUTION, AND LOGISTICS

Although union membership has dropped overall in the United States, it is still high in the transportation, distribution, and logistics industry. One reason is that transportation workers were among the first to form unions in the 1800s. Among the oldest unions is the International Brotherhood of Teamsters (IBT). This union began when drivers still used teams of horses to haul goods. Today many truck drivers belong to this union.

The Brotherhood of Locomotive Engineers (BLE) aims to protect the financial interests and safety of locomotive engineers and others employed in railway service. The United Transportation Union (UTU) represents about 125,000 active and retired railroad, bus, and mass transit workers in the United States and Canada. Another famous early union, the Brotherhood of Sleeping Car Porters, has merged with other unions to form the Transportation Communications International Union (TCU). Its 46,000 members work mostly in the railroad industry.

Ship pilots and other marine personnel may join the International Organization of Masters, Mates, and Pilots (MM&P). Those who work on docks and in warehouses may belong to the International Longshore and Warehouse Union (ILWU).

Several unions represent workers in air transportation. They include the Association of Flight Attendants, the Allied Pilots Association, and the National Air Traffic Controllers Association. Airplane mechanics, baggage handlers, reservations agents, and customer service representatives often belong to the International Association of Machinists and Aerospace Workers.

In some jobs, you may have to join a union as a condition of employment. In others, membership is optional. If you join a union, you will need to pay an initiation fee and dues. This money supports the strike fund and the work of the union. If you are thinking of joining a union, consider the costs and benefits. Examine what the union has accomplished in the past on behalf of its members.

INDUSTRY TRENDS

The transportation, distribution, and logistics industry is constantly evolving. New technology affects the way business is run. Changes in society affect how goods are shipped and how people travel. In a global economy, even events overseas can affect the way things are done at home.

Technology in the Industry

During the past few decades, technological advances have drastically changed the transportation, distribution, and logistics industry. Clients now contact companies through websites and e-mail. Companies use computers to keep track of freight, workers, schedules, and payments. Logistics managers use special software to compare costs, times, and routes in order to choose the best means of getting goods to their destinations.

SMARTPHONES AND WI-FI

Mobile computer devices are very useful in an industry that focuses on moving people and goods. Devices such as smartphones and computer tablets allow drivers to keep track of delivery locations, times, and other details. Navigation devices can direct drivers to their destination. Wi-Fi, or wireless service, allows passengers and workers to use their laptop computers as they travel. The service is now being offered on more buses and trains.

E-TICKETING AND PASSENGER INFORMATION DISPLAY SYSTEMS

Technology is making passenger travel easier. E-ticketing, or electronic ticketing, lets passengers buy tickets electronically, with no need for a physical ticket. Most airlines are moving toward a completely paperless system. Many cruise lines, train lines, and bus companies have followed their lead.

Airports and some other transportation centers now gather and display information electronically. A Passenger Information Display System (PIDS) provides arrival and departure times, gate or track numbers, and other real-time information. At transportation centers, the information is displayed on large boards and on small screens or touch-screens that passengers use. The system can display data in vehicles themselves. For example, an overhead monitor on a train might indicate the next stop and estimated arrival time. Real-time information may be accessible online by using a computer or a smartphone.

ENGINE ANALYZERS

Computer technology is now standard in motor vehicle repair. An engine analyzer, for example, is an electronic device that helps mechanics assess an engine's performance. The device looks like a large hand-held computer. It can be hooked up to various parts of a vehicle to test whether the parts are working.

Motor vehicles also have internal engine analyzers. These attach directly to the engine. They gather information about engine condition and performance. They often include an oscilloscope, which evaluates the ignition system, and a tachometer, which monitors the engine's speed.

CONVEYOR SYSTEMS AND ROBOTICS

In warehouses and distribution centers, computer controls have helped conveyor systems move goods more quickly. Robots are also increasing efficiency in warehouses. Stationary robots are used to fill orders. Gantry robots work from overhead to select cases of goods and move them to the shipping area. Robotic arms can grab specific items identified by bar code scanning. Mobile robots, which may use lasers or floor wires to move around, do many of the tasks a real person used to do.

GLOBAL POSITIONING AND INTELLIGENT TRANSPORTATION SYSTEMS

The US government has played a role in key transportation advances. The Global Positioning System (GPS), a project of the Department of Defense, is a group of satellites that pinpoint locations on Earth. Today GPS receivers aid water navigation and help taxis and delivery trucks find their way. GPS allows shippers to track vehicles and better manage their fleet.

Also useful in vehicle tracking are advances in telemetry, in which sensors on vehicles collect data and transmit it wirelessly. Such sensors are likely to play a big role in the Intelligent Transportation System (ITS) program. This joint effort between the Department of Transportation and private industry uses technology to improve the nation's surface transportation system. Its future plans include the use of wireless telemetry to create "smart" highways that provide data directly to the vehicles that travel on them.

Environmental Issues in Transportation, Distribution, and Logistics

Sustainability is another trend in business today. Sustainability refers to economic activity that does not harm the environment. The issue is of special concern to the transportation, distribution, and logistics industry, which traditionally has run on petroleum-based fuels that can harm the environment.

ALTERNATIVE FUELS AND LOWER FUEL CONSUMPTION

Efforts to make transportation "greener," or more sustainable, include the use of alternative fuels. Alternative fuels are not petroleum based. Ethanol, a kind of alcohol made from corn and other grains, may be used to fuel buses, boats, and trucks. Solar power may be used to run water vessels such as ferries. Biodiesel, diesel engine fuel made from non-petroleum oils, can be used in vehicles with diesel engines. Engines that run on electricity reduce pollution, but they have a limited range because they need recharging. A possible solution is the use of fuel cells, devices that change hydrogen and oxygen into electricity in the vehicles themselves.

Shifting to alternative fuels can be costly. By contrast, efforts to cut down on fuel use have the advantage of immediate cost savings. New technology often helps companies reduce fuel use. GPS systems on truck fleets, for instance, help avoid idle time and route errors, which waste fuel. New vehicle design features take fuel savings into account. For example, some companies are creating special truck tires that improve fuel efficiency.

"GREENER" TRANSPORTATION SYSTEMS

Some forms of transportation are "greener" than others. A big barge or a long freight train carrying cargo uses less fuel than individual trucks. A city's work force commuting on mass transit uses less fuel than individual commuters driving to work. Today many people and businesses are making "greener" transportation choices, especially when those choices save time or money. For example, rising fuel costs and traffic have increased the use of mass transit and intercity buses and trains.

Regional planners recognize these trends. Many have proposed new commuter rail systems to connect cities and suburbs. Others are considering high-speed rail between cities. Private companies are offering low-cost intercity buses.

Economic Trends in Transportation, Distribution, and Logistics

In the global economy, many goods made overseas are shipped to US markets. This increases the need for workers in the transportation, distribution, and logistics industry. Companies providing the services become more international. As a result, industry workers may find themselves in contact with workers in other countries when placing orders or scheduling deliveries.

INTERMODAL TRANSPORTATION

One important trend in the global economy is the use of intermodal transportation. Intermodal transportation means shipping freight through a of combination of truck, train, plane, or ship. Goods manufactured in Asia, for example, may be placed into containers and shipped to Seattle. The containers may then be moved to freight trains and carried to a distribution center in the Midwest. There, the goods may be unloaded onto trucks and delivered to stores.

E-COMMERCE

E-commerce is the buying and selling of goods over the Internet. It is popular with both businesses and individuals. Once goods are bought, they are shipped straight to customers from warehouses or factories. E-commerce increases the demand for carriers that can deliver small loads to individual consumers. Package delivery, air-freight express, and less-than-truckload (LTL) carriers have seen business increase as a result of e-commerce.

OUTSOURCING AND CONSULTANTS

Two ongoing workplace trends are outsourcing and the use of consultants. When companies outsource, they turn over control of some tasks to other companies. For example, manufacturers may outsource warehousing tasks. This decision can be cost-effective because not owning warehouse space saves real-estate costs. A growing trend in the global economy is to outsource certain tasks to workers abroad who work for lower pay. Such outsourcing is most likely to affect office jobs, such as phone or computer sales.

Consultants are people who provide special services. They are often hired when a project starts or when a project is being reexamined. For example, when new transportation systems are being planned, environmental consultants may be hired because of their technical knowledge.

CAREER RESOURCES

GENERAL CAREER RESOURCES

Career Clusters
www.careerclusters.org
A site featuring definitions and models of career clusters, along with information about the career clusters project.

Career Key
www.careerkey.org
A free online self-assessment that identifies students' Holland career choice personality type.

Dictionary of Occupational Titles
www.occupationalinfo.org
A searchable database of job titles and descriptions.

Mapping Your Future
www.mappingyourfuture.org
Career and education planning information for students, from middle school to adult.

Mind Tools
www.mindtools.com
A resource for developing the essential skills and techniques that will help workers excel in any chosen profession.

O*NET
http://online.onetcenter.org
An online resource center that offers skills profiles, details about hundreds of individual occupations, and crosswalks to codes from the *Dictionary of Occupational Titles*.

Occupational Outlook Handbook
www.bls.gov/oco/
The full text of the *Occupational Outlook Handbook* online provides information on education needs, earnings, prospects, descriptions, and conditions of hundreds of jobs.

Salary.com
www.salary.com
A nationwide database of salary information for hundreds of careers.

TRANSPORTATION, DISTRIBUTION, AND LOGISTICS RESOURCES

Air Transportation Association
www.airlines.org
This trade association for the world's principal airlines addresses issues such as safety, the economy, and the industry's impact on the environment.

American Trucking Association
www.truckline.com
A trade organization created to represent the interests of the trucking industry.

Association of Diesel Specialists
www.diesel.org
A federation of state lodging associations throughout the United States.

American Society of Travel Agents
astanet.com
The worldwide diesel industry's leading trade association whose members include repair shops, equipment and parts manufacturers, and mechanic training schools.

EveryTruckJob.com
www.everytruckjob.com
A trucking-industry job search site for truck drivers, mechanics, dispatchers, and others.

JobsinLogistics.com
www.jobsinlogistics.com
A career board focused on logistics jobs.

National Coalition for Aviation Education
www.aviationeducation.org
An organization representing government, industry, and labor that promotes aviation education.

National Custom Brokers and Forwarders Association of America
www.ncbfaa.org
An organization that represents workers in international trade and offers certification programs.

Professional Truck Drivers Institute
www.ptdi.org
A group that promotes truck driver training and safety and offers certification programs.

PREPARE

This section of *Career Companion: Transportation, Distribution & Logistics* provides practice of the skills you will need for any career in transportation, distribution, and logistics. It is divided into three workplace skill areas:

READING FOR INFORMATION

LOCATING INFORMATION

APPLIED MATHEMATICS

At the beginning of each section is a list of specific skills that will be presented. Also included are examples of situations in which these skills are likely to be used.

After practicing these workplace skills, you will be able to answer the following questions:

- How can I identify the main idea of a workplace document?
- What do I need to look for when following step-by-step instructions?
- How can workplace graphics help me make decisions?
- What types of calculations do I need to know to do my job?
- How can I solve problems using math operations?

Working your way through each skill area will help you prepare for a job in transportation, distribution, and logistics.

SKILLS PRACTICE

READING FOR INFORMATION

Reading for information is a key skill in the transportation, distribution, and logistics industry. You may spend your days dealing with freight or interacting with passengers one-on-one. No matter what the job, at some point you will need to read text to gather information. Before applying for a job, you will need to read a job description and understand the duties involved. You may be required to read a job application and understand the information it asks you to provide. Once hired, you may need to read the employee handbook, which lists rules and regulations for your position.

To succeed in a job, you must be able to understand the purpose of texts you encounter and identify the most important ideas and details. You must also know how to respond to them.

In the following pages, you will encounter a variety of workplace documents to read and interpret. You will also use a wide range of reading skills.

When you read a question on the following pages, think about what is being asked and how you might find the answer. Read the text carefully, focusing on the information you are asked to find or the steps you are asked to take. After you have chosen an answer, look back to make sure you have answered the question being asked.

Learning these key reading skills will speed your path to advancement in the transportation, distribution, and logistics industry.

KEY SKILLS FOR CAREER SUCCESS

Here are the topics and skills covered in this section and some examples of how you might use them to read different types of materials.

TOPIC	SKILL
Read and Understand Information in Workplace Documents	1. Identify Main Idea and Details 2. Identify Details that Are Not Clearly Stated

Example: As a logistics analyst, you may read documents that describe services offered by different shippers and determine if the details of their services match your needs.

TOPIC	SKILL
Follow Instructions from Workplace Documents	3. Understand and Apply Basic and Multi-Step Instructions 4. Apply Instructions to Unique Situations

Example: As a railroad conductor, you may need to follow a step-by-step checklist of safety rules that you would need to apply on a regular basis.

TOPIC	SKILL
Define and Use Words in the Workplace	5. Determine the Meaning of New Words 6. Understand Unique Words and Acronyms 7. Understand and Apply Technical Terms and Jargon

Example: As an automotive mechanic, you may need to read and understand technical language in a manual on how to maintain and repair a vehicle.

TOPIC	SKILL
Understand and Follow Policies and Procedures in Workplace Documents	8. Apply Workplace Policies and Procedures 9. Understand the Rationale Behind Workplace Policies

Example: As a customer service representative for a shipping company, you may receive a memo describing policy changes that you need to be able to explain to customers.

IDENTIFY MAIN IDEA AND DETAILS

When reading documents, such as memos stating changes to company safety policies, workers in the transportation, distribution, and logistics industry must be able to find the main idea. They must also find details supporting the main idea. The main idea tells what the document is about. Details provide more information that helps explain the main idea.

PASSENGER SMOKING POLICY

Smoking is prohibited in all of our trains and stations, with the following exceptions:

Station Platforms. Smoking is permitted on station platforms during longer stops. In some cases, when the train is behind schedule, if no passengers are boarding or exiting the train, certain stops might be of shorter duration or skipped altogether. Be aware that local smoking laws might prohibit smoking even on platforms. Customers are required to obey all local smoking ordinances when exiting the train at a stop.

Train Lounge Cars. Smoking is permitted only in the smoking room on train lounge cars. Note that lounge cars are not available on every train.

1. You are a conductor on a train, and are reviewing a memo regarding the smoking policy. What is the main idea of the memo?

   A. Smoking is prohibited on all trains.

   B. Smoking is permitted on all trains.

   C. Smoking is prohibited, with certain exceptions.

   D. Smoking is permitted, with certain exceptions.

   E. Smoking by train crew personnel is prohibited.

2. Which detail describes where passengers can smoke on a train?

   A. Smoking is permitted on station platforms during longer stops.

   B. Smoking is permitted only in the smoking room on train lounge cars.

   C. Be aware that local smoking laws might prohibit smoking even on platforms.

   D. Smoking is prohibited in all of our trains and stations, with the following exceptions.

   E. Note that lounge cars are not available on every train.

PRESS RELEASE

WASHINGTON - As part of its campaign to put an end to the practice of distracted driving, the U.S. Department of Transportation today proposed a new safety regulation that would specifically prohibit interstate commercial truck and bus drivers from using hand-held cell phones while operating a commercial motor vehicle (CMV).

"Every time a commercial truck or bus driver takes his or her eyes off the road to use a cell phone, even for a few seconds, the driver places everyone around them at risk," said U.S. Transportation Secretary Ray LaHood. "This proposed rule will go a long way toward keeping a driver's full attention focused on the road."

The proposed Federal Motor Carrier Safety Administration (FMCSA) rule would prohibit commercial drivers from reaching for, holding or dialing a cell phone while operating a CMV. Drivers who violate these restrictions would face federal civil penalties of up to $2,750 for each offense and disqualification of their commercial driver's license (CDL) for multiple offenses. Additionally, states would suspend a driver's CDL after two or more violations of any state law on hand-held cell phone use.

3. You are a commercial truck driver. This alert is posted at the truck yard. What is the main idea of the alert?

    A. The Department of Transportation has proposed a regulation prohibiting truck and bus drivers from using hand-held cell phones while driving.

    B. There are about four million interstate commercial truck and bus drivers in the United States.

    C. Truck and bus drivers using hand-held cell phones could be fined for each offense.

    D. Truck and bus drivers could lose their commercial license for multiple offenses.

    E. Motor carriers could face stiff penalties for allowing drivers to use hand-held cell phones.

4. Which detail in the alert refers to penalties for drivers?

    A. Drivers could have their licenses suspended for the first offense.

    B. About four million drivers would be affected by the regulation.

    C. The regulation prohibits reaching for, holding, or dialing a cell phone.

    D. Motor carriers must not allow their drivers to use hand-held cell phones.

    E. Drivers would be fined up to $2,750 for each offense.

ANSWER KEY

Item 1: **C** Smoking is prohibited, with certain exceptions.

Item 2: **B** Smoking is permitted only in the smoking room on train lounge cars.

Item 3: **A** The Department of Transportation has proposed a regulation prohibiting truck and bus drivers from using hand-held cell phones while driving.

Item 4: **E** Drivers would be fined up to $2,750 for each offense.

IDENTIFY DETAILS THAT ARE NOT CLEARLY STATED

The details in workplace documents are not always clearly stated. For example, an e-mail to delivery service truck drivers might refer to vehicle testing. Drivers would need to understand how the information relates their own vehicle. It may sometimes be necessary to infer, or make a logical guess, when a detail is suggested rather than stated.

To: All delivery drivers

From: Management

Subject: Be Prepared for Winter

Prepare a winter emergency kit for your vehicles. Supplies should include:

- At least two blankets or a sleeping bag
- Flashlight or battery-powered lantern and extra batteries
- Booster (jumper) cables
- Emergency flares
- Extra clothing, particularly boots, hats and mittens
- A steel shovel and rope to use as a lifeline
- Bottled water or juice and nonperishable high-energy foods (granola bars, raisins, nuts, peanut butter or cheese crackers)
- First-aid kit and necessary medications
- Sand or non-clumping cat litter for tire traction, if your vehicle gets stuck in snow or ice
- A cell phone and car charger

1. You are a pizza delivery driver who works in northern Minnesota. You receive an e-mail from your boss regarding winter driving preparations Why would you use cat litter?

   A. if you need extra insulation

   B. if your car gets stuck

   C. to melt snow

   D. to keep food from melting

   E. to provide fuel for a lantern

2. What might you do with a rope in snowy weather?

   A. Pull your car out of deep snow.

   B. Make emergency repairs.

   C. Create a tourniquet in case you are injured.

   D. Tie it to yourself and the car if you exit the car.

   E. Tie it around your tires for extra traction.

SECURITY CHECKPOINT ID REQUIREMENTS

All passengers over the age of 18 must present a valid federal or state-issued photo ID to security personnel. Failure to do so could result in denial of access to areas beyond the security checkpoint.

It is understood that some people do not have valid photo identification cards. This alone will not preclude a passenger from being able to board his or her flight. Voluntarily providing information to security agents that allows them to verify the identity of the passenger can be used in lieu of a federal or state-issued photo ID.

Examples of acceptable federal or state-issued photo IDs include (but are not limited to) the following:

- U.S. passport
- U.S. military ID card
- State-issued driver's license
- Department of Homeland Security "Trusted Traveler" cards
- Permanent Resident Card

All passengers entering the security checkpoints may be subject to further screening at the discretion of the screening officers. Failure to voluntarily comply with additional screenings could result in being denied access to areas beyond the security checkpoint, including being denied access to board aircraft.

3. As an airport security agent, you must verify passenger identities. What do you do if a passenger does not have a photo ID but has a birth certificate?

   A. Permit the passenger to proceed through the checkpoint.

   B. See if the name on the certificate matches the name on the ticket.

   C. Ask the passenger to provide additional information.

   D. Inform the passenger that he or she is not permitted to fly.

   E. Contact airport security to apprehend the passenger.

4. If you cannot verify a passenger's identity, what may happen?

   A. The passenger may proceed without consequence.

   B. The passenger may proceed but must undergo another ID check at the gate.

   C. The passenger may call a relative to verify his or her identity.

   D. The passenger might miss his or her flight.

   E. The passenger will be held in custody by airport security.

ANSWER KEY

Item 1:   **B** if your car gets stuck

Item 2:   **D** Tie it to yourself and the car if you exit the car.

Item 3:   **C** Ask the passenger to provide additional information.

Item 4:   **D** The passenger might miss his or her flight.

UNDERSTAND AND APPLY BASIC AND MULTI-STEP INSTRUCTIONS

It may be necessary to follow multi-step instructions in a variety of situations. A bicycle repairer may need to follow a list of posted instructions when performing a tune-up. Workers must read carefully to know when to take each step, and be able to apply the same instructions in a variety of situations.

TRAINING MANUAL: PLAN OF ACTION FOR FIRST-AID AND EMERGENCY TRANSPORT

The following points summarize the course and plan of action in rendering effective first-aid to ill and injured persons and transporting them for specialized medical care:

1. Evaluate the scene and collect all information possible on the cause of the injury or illness and the circumstances surrounding it.
2. Evaluate the injuries and establish the order that should be followed in caring for them.
3. Identify your resources and make them available for use.
4. Decide on a plan for the most effective use of available communication and transportation resources.

The school bus driver must remember that breathing, heartbeat, bleeding of a profuse nature, and shock are the four most important conditions to evaluate and must be cared for immediately if the person is to survive. Prevention of further injury in moving and transporting the victim is also extremely important.

1. As a school bus driver, you are trained in basic first-aid procedures. According to the training manual, what is the first step in developing a course of action in an emergency?

   A. Decide on a plan.

   B. Transport the victim.

   C. Identify resources.

   D. Evaluate the injuries.

   E. Evaluate the scene.

2. When should a school bus driver collect information on the cause of an injury or illness?

   A. after evaluating the injury

   B. while transporting the victim

   C. after deciding on a plan

   D. after identifying resources

   E. while evaluating the scene

HOT WEATHER DRIVING CHECKLIST

Driving in extreme weather poses risks to drivers and passengers. To reduce the number of incidents and to keep passengers safe at all times, please follow these simple directions.

- Check your radiator fluid levels. If they are low, add more radiator fluid.
- Check the air in your tires. Inflate if necessary.
- Make sure the air conditioner is working properly.
- Remind all passengers to buckle up before you begin driving.
- Make certain not to leave children in the vehicle unattended.
- Drive safely!

3. You are a van driver at a summer camp, and are reviewing the hot weather driving checklist before your first day. According to the checklist, when do you remind passengers to buckle up?

   A. before checking the tires

   B. before you begin driving

   C. after you begin driving

   D. after adding radiator fluid

   E. before inflating the tires

4. When should you add more radiator fluid?

   A. If the radiator fluid levels are low

   B. If the air conditioner is not working

   C. If the air in the tires is low

   D. After you begin driving

   E. If the heater is not working

ANSWER KEY

Item 1:   **E** Evaluate the scene.

Item 2:   **E** while evaluating the scene

Item 3:   **B** before you begin driving

Item 4:   **A** If the radiator fluid levels are low

APPLY INSTRUCTIONS TO UNIQUE SITUATIONS

Read and
Understand
Information
in Workplace
Documents

**Follow
Instructions
from
Workplace
Documents**

Define and Use
Words in the
Workplace

Understand
and Follow
Policies and
Procedures
in Workplace
Documents

A set of instructions may call for different actions in different situations. For example, a receiving clerk must choose what to do when a shipment's barcode is unreadable. The clerk must tailor the steps taken to the specific situation, so the unique circumstances must be kept in mind.

BOB'S BOOKS SHIPPING POLICY

All packages must be weighed before determining how they will be shipped.

If the package is domestic and weighs two pounds or less, ship through the United States Postal Service.

All other domestic packages ship by Rising Star Shipping Service (RSSS).

Orders sent internationally ship by USPS. Make sure that customers have accepted a shipping quote before charging their credit card.

1. You work in the shipping department of Bob's Books, a used-book seller that sells books exclusively online and so must ship all orders. You are reviewing the new shipping policy. When would you ship a package by RSSS?

   A. when a domestic package weighs less than two pounds

   B. when a domestic package weighs more than two pounds

   C. when an international package weighs more than two pounds

   D. when an international package weighs less than two pounds

   E. when a shipping quote for an international package is not accepted by the customer

2. Which condition indicates that you should check a shipping quote with customers before charging their credit card?

   A. when the package is international

   B. when the package is domestic

   C. when the package weighs less than two pounds

   D. when the package is sent by RSSS

   E. when the package is sent by USPS

COMPUTER TAGGING PURPOSE & PROCEDURE

Bar code "tagging" is the use of a numbered bar code to indicate that our computers are recorded in our equipment inventory database. The purpose of the bar codes is to ensure that all computers are accounted for, that we know where they are located and that we can keep track of our equipment.

When a new computer or piece of equipment is ordered, you must generate a bar code label the same day the order was placed. Then, put a bar code label on it as soon as it is received. If you cannot tag the item because of its size or location, you must write down the brand name of the item, the tag number associated with it and its location in the database.

3. In your job as an inventory control manager, you are required to tag all new equipment with a bar code. When do you generate the bar code label?

   A. the same day the equipment is ordered

   B. as soon as the equipment is located

   C. when the equipment is received

   D. after the equipment is tracked

   E. after the equipment is recorded

4. You receive a piece of equipment that you are unable to tag. What is one thing you need to do?

   A. Generate a new bar code number.

   B. Record it in the inventory database.

   C. Put a bar code label on it.

   D. Order another piece of equipment.

   E. Record its location in the database.

ANSWER KEY

Item 1:   **B** when a domestic package weighs more than two pounds

Item 2:   **A** when the package is international

Item 3:   **A** the same day the equipment is ordered

Item 4:   **E** Record its location in the database.

DETERMINE THE MEANING OF NEW WORDS

Read and
Understand
Information
in Workplace
Documents

Follow
Instructions
from Workplace
Documents

**Define and
Use Words in
the Workplace**

Understand
and Follow
Policies and
Procedures
in Workplace
Documents

Transportation, distribution, and logistics workers occasionally come across words whose meaning is unclear or unfamiliar. For example, someone reading a help-wanted ad for a job as a truck driver might encounter an unfamiliar word describing a task. Some words may be defined in the text, while others require the reader to discover the meaning. The context surrounding the word and the reader's background knowledge can help clarify the word's meaning.

CARGO CONTAINER SECURITY

Despite all the security changes in recent years, one area that still remains a major concern is cargo security. The volume of cargo containers entering our ports continues to remain extremely high while security remains low. The majority of cargo transport takes place via containers on ships, trains, and tractor-trailers and this movement of cargo accounts for over $1 billion in goods daily that is imported into the United States via containers. It is predicted that this number will continue to grow in the near future, resulting in over 10 million containers of freight entering the United States each year. Due to this volume, opportunities for breaches, or gaps, in security remain higher than desired. As a result, cargo security is an area which is expected to present many opportunities, and challenges, in the future.

1. As a cargo agent, you received the above reminder about the importance of container security. If one of your main concerns is a **breach** in security, what are you concerned about?

   A. the cost of security

   B. strict security

   C. a gap in security

   D. profits

   E. the number of containers

2. What is **freight**?

   A. cargo

   B. transit

   C. volume

   D. security

   E. container

COCKPIT DESIGN

The cockpit must be designed so that the required minimum flight crew can reach and operate all necessary controls and switches. Some duplication of controls and instruments may be required, depending upon the type of flight operations being carried out and the regulations under which the aircraft was certificated. The structure must be watertight to the extent that no leakage of water into the crew compartment occurs when flying through rain or snow. Noise and vibration must be within acceptable limits through design and proper insulation. For commercial transport aircraft, a lockable door must be used between the crew compartment and the passenger compartment.

3. As an aircraft mechanic, you must understand the design requirements for various parts of an aircraft. What is the **cockpit**?

   A. flight crew

   B. instrument panel

   C. passengers compartment

   D. crew compartment

   E. insulation between compartments

4. A **watertight** cockpit has what quality?

   A. It prevents leakage of rain or snow into the passenger compartment.

   B. It prevents leakage of outside air into the passenger compartment.

   C. It prevents leakage of rain or snow into the crew compartment.

   D. It prevents leakage of outside air into the crew compartment.

   E. It prevents leakage of water between the crew and passenger compartments.

ANSWER KEY

Item 1:   **C** a gap in security

Item 2:   **A** cargo

Item 3:   **D** crew compartment

Item 4:   **C** It prevents leakage of rain or snow into the crew compartment.

UNDERSTAND UNIQUE WORDS AND ACRONYMS

Acronyms (words made from the initials of several words) and abbreviations may sometimes be used without explanation in work situations. For example, an industrial safety and health engineer reading federal rules about environmental safety might come across the abbreviation CO (carbon monoxide). To understand such terms, readers may use prior knowledge or study the surrounding text to determine their meaning.

SENDING PACKAGES AS COD

Customers may pay for their order and shipping costs when their package is delivered to them using Collect On Delivery (COD). The postal service will collect payment when the package is delivered.

Make sure to fill out the COD form and enclose it with your package. The package must be mailed at the post office, so do not put it in the mail collection box.

If the customer refuses to sign for the package or the delivery is unable to be made, the package will be returned to us for an additional fee.

1. You work as a shipping clerk at an electronics warehouse, and are reviewing the shipment options. What is **COD**?

   A. cash on delivery

   B. cash on deposit

   C. collect on delivery

   D. collect on deposit

   E. customer office delivery

2. What do you need to do to send a package COD?

   A. Pay for shipping when the package is delivered.

   B. Put the package in the mail collection box.

   C. Refuse to sign for the package.

   D. Pay an additional return fee.

   E. Fill out a form and enclose it with the package.

CHOOSING A BICYCLE TIRE

Your choice of tire should be based on the type of riding surface you will typically encounter while riding your bike. For example, since bike messengers work in urban areas, they will primarily be biking on pavement. For maximum efficiency we recommend a relatively narrow and smooth tire tread pattern.

The knobby tire treads typically found on mountain bikes are ideal for off-road or dirt surfaces. These treads are wider and have more ground contact. This is useful to maintain traction on a muddy trail, but if you use a knobby tire on pavement, your ride will be slower and require more effort.

For people who will do their riding on both paved and gravel surfaces, hybrid tires may be a solution. Hybrid tires are not as knobby as off-road tires, nor are they as smooth as the road tires designed for paved roads. Hybrid tires are suitable for both pavement and gravel, but the ride won't be as comfortable.

3. You provide your own bicycle in your job as a bike messenger, and you are reviewing an article on tire tread options. What does the word **encounter** mean in this passage?

    A. experience

    B. engage in conflict with

    C. find

    D. clash with

    E. meet as an adversary

4. What does the word **ride** refer to in the second paragraph of this article?

    A. the tire

    B. the trip

    C. the tread

    D. the trail

    E. the route

ANSWER KEY

Item 1:   **C** collect on delivery

Item 2:   **E** Fill out a form and enclose it with the package.

Item 3:   **A** experience

Item 4:   **B** the trip

UNDERSTAND AND APPLY TECHNICAL TERMS AND JARGON

Workers in the transportation, distribution, and logistics industry need to understand workplace documents that use technical terms and jargon, or industry-specific language. Automotive mechanics may read technical terms in a car repair manual. They must be able to interpret the meanings of these terms and apply them to the situation at hand.

SPECIAL AIRWORTHINESS INFORMATION BULLETIN

This Special Airworthiness Information Bulletin is intended to alert owners, operators, and mechanics of the risk of the development of fuel vapor in the Acme H233 helicopters when operated at high temperatures.

During the helicopter's ferry flight from Acme's factory in Oregon to Customers in California, the pilot reported temporary power loss while flying through an area where air temperature was recorded at 103 °F. Tests conducted to replicate the situation identified possible fuel vapor forming in the fuel lines when air temperature exceeds 100 °F. The vapor forms when the air heats the fuel lines sufficiently to cause the fuel to transition from a liquid to a gaseous state. It has been determined that the cause of the formation of fuel vapor is poorly insulated fuel lines.

All pilots, mechanics, and owners should inspect fuel lines on all Acme H233 helicopters for signs of inadequate insulation and repair as needed. Pilots should also restrict their flights when the air temperature exceeds 100 °F until modifications are made. If fuel vapor is suspected while in flight, reduce altitude and conclude flight operations as soon as possible.

1. You are a mechanic who receives service bulletins via e-mail from the regional director. In the bulletin, what does the term **airworthiness** mean?

   A. cost-effectiveness

   B. air quality

   C. part design quality

   D. pilot quality

   E. fitness for flying

2. Fuel lines should be inspected to help avoid the formation of fuel vapor. When **fuel vapor** forms, what happens?

   A. The temperature exceeds 100°F.

   B. The fuel ignites, resulting in a dangerous situation for the pilot.

   C. The pilot cannot increase altitude due to low fuel levels.

   D. The fuel goes from a liquid state to a gaseous state.

   E. The fuel lines become clogged.

To: All Diesel Mechanics

From: Maintenance Manager

Subject: Biodiesel Information

As we move to using a fleet of trucks that run on biodiesel, it is important that we all familiarize ourselves with what biodiesel is and what it's made of. Please read the following information provided to us by the Department of Energy to better understand biodiesel fuels.

Biodiesel is a *liquid fuel* made from vegetable oils, recycled cooking grease, and animal fats. In the United States, most biodiesel is made from soybean oil, whereas in Europe, rapeseed oil (canola) is the commonest feedstock. Biodiesel is made through a chemical process called transesterification, a process in which the oil reacts with alcohol in the presence of a catalyst leaving behind two products - methyl esters (biodiesel), and glycerin (a valuable byproduct used in soaps).

Currently, biodiesel is blended with petroleum-based diesel, at up to 20% (called B20 blend stock), for trucks and heavy-duty vehicles. It is manufactured in accordance with specification ASTM D6751. Biodiesel can be considered a cleaner-burning fuel as it contains virtually none of the nitrogen or aromatic compounds, such as benzene, typically found in petroleum-based fuels, and could reduce the levels of emissions upon combustion. It has a very low sulfur content, typically less than 25 parts per million (ppm).

3. You are a diesel engine specialist. Your supervisor wants to convert several trucks to biodiesel and sent this article to you. Why is it important that biodiesel contains virtually no **aromatic compounds**?

   A. biodiesel is expensive to produce

   B. biodiesel burns cleaner than petroleum-based fuels

   C. biodiesel can be made from a variety of sources

   D. biodiesel can be used to make glycerin

   E. biodiesel is cheaper to produce

4. Biodiesel is produced through a process called **transesterification** What is required for this process to occur?

   A. glycerin and alcohol

   B. glycerin, soap, and vegetable oil

   C. oil, alcohol, and a catalyst

   D. methyl esters and a catalyst

   E. methyl esters and vegetable oil

ANSWER KEY

Item 1:   **E** fitness for flying

Item 2:   **D** The fuel goes from a liquid state to a gaseous state.

Item 3:   **B** biodiesel burns cleaner than petroleum-based fuels

Item 4:   **C** oil, alcohol, and a catalyst

SKILL

8

Read and
Understand
Information
in Workplace
Documents

Follow
Instructions
from Workplace
Documents

Define and Use
Words in the
Workplace

**Understand
and Follow
Policies and
Procedures
in Workplace
Documents**

APPLY WORKPLACE POLICIES AND PROCEDURES

Many transportation, distribution, and logistics workers receive a policies and procedures manual when they begin work. It is important not just to understand the text of the manual, but to also apply the policies to their actual work situation. For example, understanding the reasons for a warehouse's workplace safety principles can help workers deal with potentially dangerous events.

QUICK COURIER'S SHIPPING POLICY ON DANGEROUS GOODS

Dangerous goods are materials or substances that might cause harm to people or property.

Quick Courier does not allow the shipping of dangerous items. Some dangerous items are common products not dangerous during regular use, but they can be dangerous when mailed due to vibration, temperature changes and changes in atmospheric pressure.

We do not ship the following items:

Aerosols	Chlorine	Flea collars or sprays	
Batteries	Dry ice	Glue	Nail polish
Bleach	Fireworks	Matches	Paint

If you have any questions about an item not listed above, please contact your supervisor.

1. As a shipping clerk at a parcel courier company, you are reviewing the shipping policy on dangerous goods. What is the purpose of prohibiting the shipment of dangerous goods?

   A. It would cost the company too much money.

   B. The items would need to be shipped separately.

   C. The items might break during shipment if not packaged well.

   D. The items could explode or hurt somebody.

   E. The items are too bulky to mail.

2. Why would you need to contact your supervisor with questions?

   A. to see if an item is on the list

   B. to see if an unlisted item is dangerous

   C. to see if he or she has questions

   D. to hand him or her any questionable packages

   E. to ask him or her if the policy has changed

PILOT RESPONSIBILITY AND AUTHORITY.

The pilot has primary responsibility for safety. The pilot will refuse to deviate from approved mission profile except for safety of flight and may refuse to pilot any flight, if, in the pilot's opinion, conditions exist which make the flight unsafe.

Pilots are responsible for:

1. Ensuring the administration, safety, and maintenance of aircraft are in accordance with FAA regulations.

2. Determining that the aircraft is airworthy and that required periodic maintenance checks are carried out.

3. Ensuring that all major repairs and overhauls on aircraft are accomplished in commercial shops certified by FAA for each individual aircraft. Repair work may also be performed by Reclamation personnel provided they are certified by FAA.

4. Interpreting and keeping current with FAA regulations and informed of hazards of flight.

5. Being aware of and conforming to the Department of the Interior, Federal Aviation Regulations of the FAA, Reclamation Directives, Notices to Airmen, and the regulations and directives of other applicable authorities, including those relating to use for official purposes only and the transportation of unofficial passengers.

3. You are a pilot who flies a small airplane. A government agency hires you to make flights to help conduct a scientific survey. A month before the flight, your plane's rudder stops working. A repair would take one week. According to the policy above, what should you do?

   A. Inform the client that the aircraft is not airworthy.

   B. Tell the client the aircraft can't be fixed in time for the flight.

   C. Have the aircraft repaired by an FAA-certified repair facility.

   D. Have the aircraft repaired by any reputable repair facility.

   E. Repair the rudder yourself.

4. On the morning of a flight the weather is stormy and visibility is poor. What should you do?

   A. Proceed with the flight as scheduled.

   B. Proceed with the flight only if the passengers sign safety waivers.

   C. Ensure the aircraft has enough fuel to land elsewhere.

   D. Consult the FAA for its opinion on the safety of the conditions.

   E. Postpone the flight until you decide that conditions are safe.

ANSWER KEY

Item 1: **D** The items could explode or hurt somebody.

Item 2: **B** to see if an unlisted item is dangerous

Item 3: **C** Have the aircraft repaired by an FAA-certified repair facility.

Item 4: **E** Postpone the flight until you decide that conditions are safe.

Read and
Understand
Information
in Workplace
Documents

Follow
Instructions
from Workplace
Documents

Define and Use
Words in the
Workplace

**Understand
and Follow
Policies and
Procedures
in Workplace
Documents**

UNDERSTAND THE RATIONALE BEHIND WORKPLACE POLICIES

As with any industry, workplace policies in the transportation, distribution, and logistics industry are created for a reason. A billing clerk in a shipping company must be able to explain billing policies to customers. This knowledge helps workers to ensure the policies are being followed in the proper manner.

MEMO

To: All Warehouse Employees

Re: Safe Lifting Procedures

Given the recent increase in back injuries among your fellow workers, I must remind you of our safety procedures. All employees must practice safe lifting methods at all times. Here are some tips.

- If a box appears too heavy or unwieldy, get a partner to help you lift it.
- Keep your feet shoulder width apart while lifting.
- Keep one foot next to the object you are lifting and one foot behind it.
- Do not stoop down to pick up the package. Bend your knees instead.
- Keep your arms and elbows close to your body while you are lifting the package.
- Carry the package close to your body.
- Pay attention to where you are going.
- When lowering the package, bend your knees rather than stooping.

1. As a warehouse worker at a shipping center, you must often lift heavy objects. According to the memo, What is a likely reason for using a shoulder-width stance while lifting?

   A. It provides more balance.

   B. It helps others see you.

   C. It helps you see over the top of the box.

   D. It makes stooping easier.

   E. It is quicker.

2. What is the rationale behind the requirement that heavy or unwieldy boxes be lifted by two people?

   A. It prevents damage to the contents.

   B. All employees carry heavy boxes.

   C. It is a safety precaution.

   D. Not everyone has to follow the requirement.

   E. It ensures people work together.

COMPLIANCE POLICY

Civil penalty sanctions should not be recommended for conditions that the railroad could not have prevented through use of due diligence, provided those conditions occurred subsequent to a previous inspection or test of the system. Conditions that arise through no fault on the part of the railroad include, for example:

- Gate arm breakage.
- Lamp outage or damage to flashing light units due to mechanical damage.

In other cases, normal operation of the system may result in occasional component failure or lack of adjustment that is not predictable or reasonably preventable, for example:

- Lamp outage due to normal burn out of filament, where outages represent failure at an expected rate due to expired service life.
- Switch circuit controller connection loose at time of quarterly inspection.

In individual cases such as those cited above, the inspector should record a defect and the railroad will be expected to promptly remedy the condition as required by Section 234.207.

3. You are a railroad inspector. Why does this compliance policy list examples of railroad defects?

   A. To show conditions warranting sanctions for noncompliance.

   B. To show when civil penalty sanctions are not appropriate.

   C. To ensure enforcement of safety regulations for rail crossings.

   D. To ensure cars and pedestrians follow safety regulations.

   E. To show the parts of a crossing that are likely to need inspection.

4. How does this policy affect your job?

   A. You must record more types of railroad defects than before.

   B. You cannot use sanctions to enforce safety regulations.

   C. You must assess sanctions for all defects, regardless of the cause.

   D. You must use good judgment when assessing sanctions.

   E. You must work harder to enforce railroad safety regulations.

ANSWER KEY

Item 1: **A** It provides more balance.

Item 2: **C** It is a safety precaution.

Item 3: **B** To show when civil penalty sanctions are not appropriate.

Item 4: **D** You must use good judgment when assessing sanctions.

SKILLS PRACTICE

LOCATING INFORMATION

To succeed in a transportation, distribution, and logistics career, you must be able to effectively locate information. Information comes in a variety of forms, including tables, graphs, maps, and diagrams. You may need to locate this information in graphics on a computer screen, in a document, or even posted on a bulletin board or wall.

Locating information means more than just finding it. It also means understanding it and making use of it in the job you do each day. It may also mean finding missing information and adding it to a document.

On the following pages, you will encounter a variety of workplace graphics. You will be asked to find important information in these graphics. In some cases you must interpret information in these graphics. For example, you may need to compare data, summarize it, or sort through distracting information.

When you read a question on the following pages, think about what is being asked and how you might find the answer. Look carefully at the graphic, focusing on the information you are asked to find or the steps you are asked to take. After you have chosen an answer, look back to make sure you have answered the question being asked.

Learning these key locating information skills will speed your path to advancement in the transportation, distribution, and logistics industry.

KEY SKILLS FOR CAREER SUCCESS

Here are the topics and skills covered in this section and some examples of how you might use them to read different types of graphics.

TOPIC	SKILL
Locate and Compare Information in Graphics	1. Find Information in Workplace Graphics 2. Enter Information into Workplace Graphics

Example: As a billing clerk, you may need to sift through different work orders and shipping documents to prepare a complete bill for a customer.

Analyze Trends in Workplace Graphics	3. Identify Trends in Workplace Graphics 4. Compare Trends in Workplace Graphics

Example: As a logistics manager, you may need to review charts that show how distribution needs are changing over time.

Use Information from Workplace Graphics	5. Summarize Information in Workplace Graphics 6. Make Decisions Based on Workplace Graphics

Example: As an air traffic controller, you will need to decide what instructions to give to pilots based on information on your radar screen and other monitors.

Locate and
Compare
Information
in Graphics

Analyze Trends
in Workplace
Graphics

Use Information
from Workplace
Graphics

FIND INFORMATION IN WORKPLACE GRAPHICS

When reading a workplace graphic, transportation, distribution, and logistics workers must know what information to look for. For example, a truck loader may study a diagram showing how to stack items to use space efficiently. Workers must be able to sift through irrelevant or distracting information to find what is needed.

Charges For Shipping And Handling

If your order total is	Add
$0.00 – $50.00	$8.00
$50.01 – $100.00	$10.00
$100.01 – $200.00	$15.00
$200.01 – $500.00	$20.00
$500.01 – $1,000.00	$25.00
$1,000.01 +	$40.00

1. In your job as a shipping clerk, you must add a shipping and handling fee to each item you are going to ship. The charge is based on the value of the item. If an item is valued at $500, what amount do you add for shipping and handling?

   A. $8

   B. $10

   C. $15

   D. $20

   E. $25

2. You are shipping an item valued at $1,500. What is the fee for shipping and handling?

   A. $20

   B. $25

   C. $40

   D. $60

   E. $80

FEDERAL HAZARDOUS MATERIALS TRANSPORTATION LAW

Contents
49 U.S.C.
SUBTITLE III — GENERAL AND INTERMODAL PROGRAMS
CHAPTER 51 — TRANSPORTATION OF HAZARDOUS MATERIAL[1]

[1] As amended by H.R.3 - SAFETEA-LU (Public Law 109-59, 119 Stat. 1144, August 10, 2005)

3. In your job as a truck loader, you are required to handle hazardous materials. Your boss asks you to review the Hazardous Materials Transportation Law. In which section would you find the handling criteria for hazardous materials?

A. Section 5106

B. Section 5112

C. Section 5127

D. Section 7128

E. Section 7131

4. What would you find in Section 5104?

A. information on civil penalties

B. information on the incident response system

C. information on special permits and exclusions

D. information on the air transportation of ionizing radiation material

E. information on representation and tampering of hazardous material

ANSWER KEY

Item 1: **D** $20

Item 2: **C** $40

Item 3: **A** Section 5106

Item 4: **E** information on representation and tampering of hazardous material

SKILL

2

Locate and
Compare
Information
in Graphics

Analyze Trends
in Workplace
Graphics

Use Information
from Workplace
Graphics

ENTER INFORMATION INTO WORKPLACE GRAPHICS

It may be necessary at times to add information to a workplace graphic. As a bus driver, you may need to enter your arrival time at your final stop in a detailed log, for example. Knowing where to add this information is an important skill in this industry.

Inventory Information Chart

	A	B	C	D	E
1	Style #	Color	Size	Season	SKU
2	14789	Black	5	Fall 2010	14789-001-Q10-5
3	14789	Black	7	Fall 2010	14789-001-Q10-7
4	14789	Black	11	Fall 2010	14789-001-Q10-11
5	14789	Black	13	Fall 2010	14789-001-Q10-13
6	14789	Black	15	Fall 2010	14789-001-Q10-15
7	14789	Red	5	Fall 2010	14789-002-Q10-5
8	14789	Red	7	Fall 2010	14789-002-Q10-7
9	14789	Red	11	Fall 2010	14789-002-Q10-11
10	14789	Red	13	Fall 2010	14789-002-Q10-13
11	14789	Red	15	Fall 2010	14789-002-Q10-15
12	14791	Tan	S	Fall 2010	14791-003-Q10-S
13	14791	Tan	M	Fall 2010	14791-003-Q10-M
14	14791	Tan	L	Fall 2010	14791-003-Q10-L
15	14791	Tan	XL	Fall 2010	14791-003-Q10-XL
16	14791	Blue	S	Fall 2010	14791-004-Q10-S
17	14791	Blue	M	Fall 2010	14791-004-Q10-M
18	14791	Blue	L	Fall 2010	14791-004-Q10-L

1. You work as a category manager and are asked to look up Stock-Keeping Unit (SKU) # 14791-003-Q10-S. What are the color and size of this item?

   A. Black, size 7

   B. Red, size 11

   C. Red, size S

   D. Tan, size S

   E. Red, size 15

2. You decide to send more shipments for items of sizes 11, 13, and 15. Which items do you send?

   A. 1, 3, 4, 9, 11, 14, 15, 16

   B. 4, 5, 6, 9, 10, 11

   C. 2, 3, 5, 8, 13, 16, 18

   D. 1, 2, 8, 12, 17

   E. 5, 6, 7, 10, 11, 15, 18

SHIPPER'S EXPORT DECLARATION

1. U.S. PRINCIPAL PARTY IN INTEREST (USPPI)(Complete name and address)

ZIP CODE

2. DATE OF EXPORTATION

3. TRANSPORTATION REFERENCE NO.

USPPI'S EIN (IRS) OR ID NO.

c. PARTIES TO TRANSACTION
☐ Related ☐ Non-related

4. ULTIMATE CONSIGNEE *(Complete name and address)*

INTERMEDIATE CONSIGNEE *(Complete name and address)*

5. FORWARDING AGENT *(Complete name and address)*

5. FORWARDING AGENT'S EIN (IRS) NO.

6. POINT (STATE) OF ORIGIN OR FTZ NO.

7. COUNTRY OF ULTIMATE DESTINATION

8. LOADING PIER *(Vessel only)*

9. METHOD OF TRANSPORTATION *(Specify)*

14. CARRIER IDENTIFICATION CODE

15. SHIPMENT REFERENCE NO.

10. EXPORTING CARRIER

11. PORT OF EXPORT

16. ENTRY NUMBER

17. HAZARDOUS MATERIALS
☐ Yes ☐ No

12. PORT OF UNLOADING *(Vessel and air only)*

13. CONTAINERIZED *(Vessel only)*
☐ Yes ☐ No

18. IN BOND CODE

19. ROUTED EXPORT TRANSACTION
☐ Yes ☐ No

20. SCHEDULE B DESCRIPTION OF COMMODITIES *(Use columns 22–24)*

D/F or M (21)	SCHEDULE B NUMBER (22)	QUANTITY – SCHEDULE B UNIT(S) (23)	SHIPPING WEIGHT (Kilograms) (24)	VIN/PRODUCT NUMBER/ VEHICLE TITLE NUMBER (25)	VALUE (U.S. dollars, omit cents) (Selling price or cost if not sold) (26)

3. In your job in warehouse distribution, you ship products to China. In which section would you write "China"?

   A. 2
   B. 7
   C. 8
   D. 20
   E. 25

4. You are shipping items on January 19, 2011. In which section would you indicate this?

   A. 2
   B. 8
   C. 12
   D. 18
   E. 29

ANSWER KEY

Item 1: **D** Tan, size S
Item 2: **B** 4, 5, 6, 9, 10, 11
Item 3: **B** 7
Item 4: **A** 2

SKILL

3

Locate and
Compare
Information
in Graphics

**Analyze
Trends in
Workplace
Graphics**

Use Information
from Workplace
Graphics

IDENTIFY TRENDS IN WORKPLACE GRAPHICS

Transportation, distribution, and logistics workers must sometimes analyze graphics to identify trends. They might search for data that has changed over time. A warehouse manager might note that shipments from a certain location are being delivered more slowly than previously. Being able to identify common trends from several pieces of data can help with a variety of jobs in this industry.

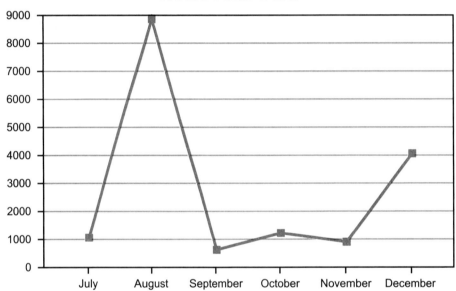

Notebooks Sold

1. As an inventory control analyst, you are looking at notebook sales to predict inventory needs for next year. What conclusions can you draw from the sales data?

    A. Notebook sales are relatively consistent throughout the year.

    B. Notebook sales increase dramatically before school starts in September.

    C. Notebook sales fluctuate unpredictably year-round.

    D. Notebook sales are highest in October.

    E. Notebook sales are lowest in December.

2. Which two months would require prioritizing the restocking of notebooks?

    A. October and November

    B. July and August

    C. September and November

    D. August and December

    E. October and December

Gold exploration activity by region, 1995 through 2004

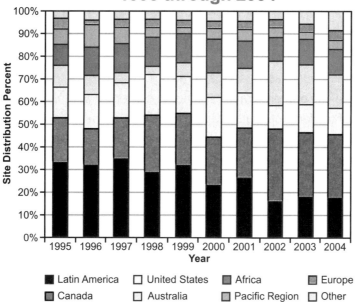

■ Latin America   □ United States   ▨ Africa   ▨ Europe
▨ Canada   □ Australia   ▨ Pacific Region   □ Other

3. You work as a logistics director for an international mining equipment company. You coordinate the transportation and deployment of equipment for various mining sites around the world. You are reviewing global mining trends to better anticipate future needs. What is the trend in gold exploration?

A. Gold exploration has generally increased in Canada, but decreased in Latin America.

B. Gold exploration is increasing in the U.S. and Australia.

C. Gold exploration has dramatically decreased in Canada and Australia.

D. Gold exploration has expanded in the U.S., but decreased in Africa.

E. Gold exploration has increased significantly in Africa and the Pacific Region.

4. Based on the trends in gold exploration in this chart, in which two regions will you probably deploy less equipment in the future?

A. Latin America and Europe

B. Canada and Africa

C. Australia and the United States

D. Australia and Canada

E. Europe and the Pacific Region

ANSWER KEY

Item 1:   **B** Notebook sales increase dramatically before school starts in September.

Item 2:   **D** August and December

Item 3:   **A** Gold exploration has generally increased in Canada, but decreased in Latin America.

Item 4:   **E** Europe and the Pacific Region

SKILL

4

Locate and
Compare
Information
in Graphics

**Analyze
Trends in
Workplace
Graphics**

Use Information
from Workplace
Graphics

COMPARE TRENDS IN WORKPLACE GRAPHICS

When reviewing workplace graphics, it may be necessary to compare information in one or more graphics. A home delivery driver might compare a schedule of truck maintenance with his own delivery schedule. The driver must know how different graphics relate to each other, and be able to compare information and trends within them.

Inventory and Sales for "Twin" Sofa Bed, by Month

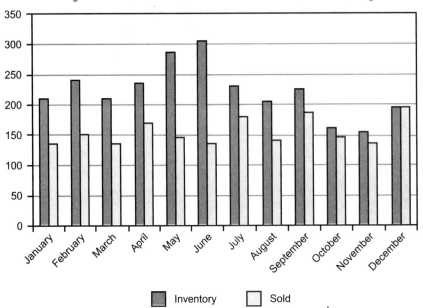

1. You work as a supply chain manager for a national retail furniture store. You are reviewing last year's sales and inventory data for a specific sofa bed. You try to avoid having inventory levels that are too high. In which month were inventory levels at least twice as high as sales?

   A. February

   B. June

   C. July

   D. August

   E. November

2. What is the trend in the relationship between inventory levels and sales?

   A. Inventory and sales figures were close to each other year-round.

   B. Inventory and sales figures were never close at any time of year.

   C. Inventory and sales figures were very different early in the year but were close late in the year.

   D. Inventory and sales figures differed greatly part of the year but were closest in the January.

   E. Inventory and sales figures were about the same during much of the year but were very far apart in the last three months.

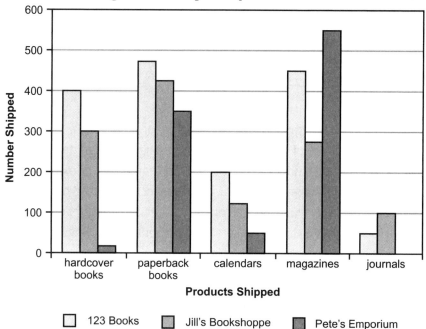

Average Monthly Shipments to Bookstore

Products Shipped

☐ 123 Books   ▨ Jill's Bookshoppe   ▧ Pete's Emporium

3. You work as a warehouse manager in a book distribution center, and are reviewing past orders from three local bookstores. Based on the data, which comparison is true?

    A. Jill's Bookshoppe orders more hardcover books than the other bookstores.

    B. Pete's Emporium orders more calendars than the other bookstores.

    C. 123 Books orders more books overall than the other bookstores.

    D. Jill's Bookshoppe orders more journals than any other item.

    E. Pete's Emporium orders more paperback books than 123 Books.

4. Which item does Pete's Emporium order more than any other?

    A. Hardcover books

    B. Paperback books

    C. Calendars

    D. Magazines

    E. Journals

ANSWER KEY

Item 1: **B** June

Item 2: **C** Inventory and sales figureswere very different early in the year but were close late in the year.

Item 3: **C** 123 Books orders more books overall than the other bookstores.

Item 4: **D** Magazines

Locate and
Compare
Information
in Graphics

Analyze Trends
in Workplace
Graphics

**Use
Information
from
Workplace
Graphics**

SUMMARIZE INFORMATION IN WORKPLACE GRAPHICS

When workers look at a graphic such as a diagram or a bar graph, they need to analyze and make sense of the information. It may be necessary to summarize the information, or boil it down to the most important facts. For example, a transportation planner might analyze two designs for a proposed highway off-ramp and summarize the key features of each one for an advisory committee. Being able to summarize allows workers to make sense of varying information.

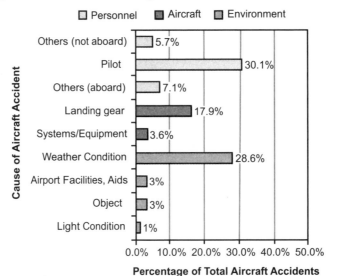

Top Factors in Passenger Aircraft Accidents in 2006

1. As an airport safety supervisor, you manage only non-flight personnel. Considering this, which statistic above should concern you the most?

   A. Weather conditions were a factor in 28.6% of accidents.

   B. Landing gear was a factor in 17.9% of accidents

   C. Non-aircraft personnel were a factor in 5.7% of accidents.

   D. Systems and equipment were a factor in 3.6% of accidents.

   E. On-board, non-pilot personnel were factors in 7.1% of accidents.

2. What can you conclude about environmental factors in accidents?

   A. Weather condition is the least frequent aircraft accident cause.

   B. Airport facilities and objects on runways cause accidents equally.

   C. Light condition is the leading factor in aircraft accidents.

   D. Environmental factors cause fewer accidents than personnel.

   E. Weather condition contributes to more accidents than pilots.

WARNING DEVICE COMPARISON: CROSSINGS WITH WHISTLE BANS VS. TOTAL CROSSINGS IN U.S.

Crossings with Whistle Bans:

Warning Device	Number of Crossings	Share of Total Crossings
Gates	1027	50.7%
Flashing Lights	450	22.2%
Passive	490	24.2%
None	60	2.9%
TOTAL:	2027	100.0%

Public Crossings in U.S. (as of 2002)

Gates	35,369	23.2%
Flashers	31,357	20.4%
Crossbucks	81,624	53.1%
None/Other	5076	3.3%
TOTAL:	153,446	100.0%

Source: Federal Railroad Administration

3. You are a locomotive engineer for a major railroad line. You are reviewing safety warning devices used at railroad crossings in light of some recent incidents in areas with whistle bans. Based on the graphic, what do you conclude about railroad crossings that use gates as warning devices?

A. The same rate of crossings have gates whether they are in areas with whistle bans or not.

B. Flashing lights make better warning devices than gates at railroad crossings.

C. All incidents occurred at railroad crossings that contain no warning devices.

D. Passive warning devices are in greater use in areas without whistle bans than in areas with whistle bans.

E. It is more important that railroad crossings in areas with whistle bans have gates than in areas without whistle bans.

4. Both passive warning devices and crossbucks in the graphic consist of signs without the use of flashing lights or gates. What can you conclude about the use of passive warning devices and crossbucks?

A. Both crossbucks and passive devices are used at about the same rate in areas with whistle bans and in areas without whistle bans.

B. Passive devices are just as effective as flashing lights and gates.

C. Crossbucks are used more often in areas without whistle bans than passive devices are used in areas with whistle bans.

D. You are more likely to see no warning devices in use at all than to see passive devices or crossbucks.

E. Passive devices are used more often in areas with whistle bans than crossbucks are used in areas without whistle bans.

ANSWER KEY

Item 1: **C** Personnel not aboard the aircraft were a factor in 5.7% of accidents.

Item 2: **B** Airport facilities and objects on the runway cause accidents equally.

Item 3: **E** It is more important that railroad crossings in areas with whistle bans have gates than in areas without whistle bans.

Item 4: **C** Crossbucks are used more often in areas without whistle bans than passive devices are used in areas with whistle bans.

SKILL

6

Locate and
Compare
Information
in Graphics

Analyze Trends
in Workplace
Graphics

**Use
Information
from
Workplace
Graphics**

MAKE DECISIONS BASED ON WORKPLACE GRAPHICS

After analyzing the information in a workplace graphic, the next step is often to make a decision or take action as a result of the analysis. In the transportation, distribution, and logistics industry, after reviewing charts showing industrial accidents, an industrial safety and health engineer might change the workflow processes within a warehouse. Making the right decisions based on graphical information can help a business operate more safely.

When to Record Fuel Changeover Operations in Your Ship's Logbooks

When a record of fuel changeover operation is required		What is required to be recorded				
		Time	Date	Position of ship	Volume in each tank with fuel oil not exceeding 1.50% Sulphur	Volume in each tank with fuel oil not exceeding .10% Sulphur
Before entry into a SECA	Operation is completed	✔	✔	✔	✔	
Following departure from SECA	Operation commences	✔	✔	✔	✔	
Following arrival of ship at berth	Operation commences and is completed	✔	✔			✔
Before departure of ship from birth	Operation commences and is completed	✔	✔			✔

1. As a captain of a large cargo ship, you must follow certain environmental regulations. According to the memo, when do you log the volume of fuel not exceeding 1.50% Sulphur?

   A. after entering a Sulphur Emission Control Area

   B. only after leaving a Sulphur Emission Control Area

   C. before entering and after leaving a Sulphur Emission Control Area

   D. after arriving at berth and before departing from berth

   E. before arriving at berth and after departing from berth

2. Which of the following is the complete list of information you must record in the ship's log after your ship arrives at its berth?

   A. Time

   B. Time and date

   C. Time, date, and position of ship

   D. Time, date, and volume of fuel not exceeding 0.10% Sulphur

   E. Time, date, and volume of fuel not exceeding 1.50% Sulphur

TABLE 1. FAA/INDUSTRY AGREED
UPON BRAKING ACTION DEFINITIONS

Braking Action		Estimated Correlations		
Term	Definition	Runway Surface Condition	ICAO	
			Code	Mu
Good		• Water depth of 1/8" or less • Dry snow less than ¾" in depth • Compacted snow with OAT at or below 15 ºC	5	40 & above
Good to Medium			4	39–36
Medium (Fair)		• Dry snow ¾" or greater in depth • Sanded snow • Sanded ice • Compacted snow with OAT above 15 ºC	3	35–30
Medium to Poor			2	29–26
Poor		• Wet snow • Slush • Water depth more than 1/8" • Ice (not melting)	1	25–21
Nil		• Ice (melting) • Wet Ice	9	20 & below

NOTE: Conditions specified as "Nil" braking action are not considered safe. Do not operate on surfaces reported as Nil. Further, the ICAO term "Unreliable" approximates Nil.

Runway	Current Surface Condition
Runway A	Dry snow 1" deep
Runway B	Wet snow and slush
Runway C	Ice (not melting)
Runway D	Wet and/or melting ice
Runway E	Dry snow ½" deep

3. As an airport operations manager, you assess runway safety. Given the conditions above, which runway's braking conditions are best?

   A. Runway A

   B. Runway B

   C. Runway C

   D. Runway D

   E. Runway E

4. If the safest runway is unavailable, which is the next best choice?

   A. Runway A

   B. Runway B

   C. Runway C

   D. Runway D

   E. Runway E

ANSWER KEY

Item 1:   **C** before entering and after leaving a Sulphur Emission Control Area

Item 2:   **D** Time, date, and volume of fuel not exceeding 0.10% Sulphur

Item 3:   **E** Runway E

Item 4:   **A** Runway A

SKILLS PRACTICE

APPLIED MATHEMATICS

Using applied mathematics will also help you succeed in the transportation, distribution, and logistics career cluster. The mathematics required for this cluster can be complex. As a vessel traffic control specialist, you may need to use several mathematical steps to coordinate traffic in shipping lanes safely. Other skills are very simple, such as counting boxes on a palette. Some key skills include multiplying and dividing, finding percentages, and adding fractions.

On the following pages, you will encounter a variety of applied math problems. Each item describes a real-life situation in a transportation, distribution, and logistics career. You will be asked to solve the problems by applying your mathematical skills. You may need to use arithmetic, geometry, or measurement skills, for example.

When you read a question on the following pages, think about what is being asked and how you might find the answer. Read the text carefully, focusing on the information you are asked to find or the steps you are asked to take. After you have chosen an answer, look back to make sure you have answered the question being asked.

By learning and practicing these key mathematical skills, you will put yourself in a better position to succeed in the transportation, distribution, and logistics industry.

KEY SKILLS FOR CAREER SUCCESS

Here are the topics and skills covered in this section and some examples how you might use them to solve workplace problems.

TOPIC	SKILL
Perform Basic Arithmetic Calculations to Solve Workplace Problems	1. Solve Problems with Whole Numbers and Negative Numbers 2. Use Fractions, Decimals, and Percentages to Solve Workplace Problems

Example: As a flight navigator, you may need to calculate changes in the amounts of fuel a plane is using based on changes in speed.

Apply Computations to Solve Workplace Problems	3. Use General Problem Solving 4. Solve Problems in Geometry

Example: As a freight, stock, or material mover, you may need to calculate the number of crates that will fit in an area based on the measurements of that area.

Solve Measurement Problems	5. Calculate with Conversions and Formulas 6. Manipulate Formulas to Solve Problems

Example: As a freight forwarder, you may need to convert prices from one currency into another.

Make Spending Decisions to Solve Workplace Problems	7. Calculate Costs and Discounts 8. Make Consumer Comparisons

Example: As a regional planner, you may need to compare the cost of using different contractors and different materials in making plans for a new roadway.

SOLVE PROBLEMS WITH WHOLE NUMBERS AND NEGATIVE NUMBERS

Perform Basic Arithmetic Calculations to Solve Workplace Problems

Apply Computations to Solve Workplace Problems

Solve Measurement Problems

Make Spending Decisions to Solve Workplace Problems

Addition, subtraction, multiplication, and division of whole numbers are important skills in any career cluster, and transportation, distribution, and logistics is no exception. A cargo or freight agent, for example, must be able to add to find the total number of packages being shipped to one place.

1. As a driver for a delivery service, you arrive at your office and review your delivery route to ensure you have enough gasoline in your truck to drive the day's route. You see that you have 3 deliveries to make today. Delivery 1 is located 14 miles from your present location. Delivery 2 is 19 miles from the first delivery location. Delivery 3 is 7 miles from the Delivery 2 location. The Delivery 3 location is 36 miles from your office. How many miles will you drive to complete the three deliveries and return to the office?

   A. 55

   B. 70

   C. 76

   D. 80

   E. 93

2. You are the assistant manager of a delivery service. The manager has purchased a new van for the business. The manager purchased the van because the expected mileage for the van is 13 miles per gallon for city driving and 17 miles per gallon for highway driving, a big improvement over the old delivery van. You are recalculating your fuel budget and need to know the new van's gas mileage. The van has a 35-gallon gas tank. If your deliveries are all within the city, how many miles can be driven on each tank of gas?

   A. 350

   B. 405

   C. 440

   D. 455

   E. 525

3. Your company asked you, the warehouse assistant, to hire summer interns from a local high school. In September, seven of these interns will return to school. If there are currently 23 workers employed at the warehouse, how many will remain after the students return to school?

   A. 12

   B. 15

   C. 16

   D. 18

   E. 30

4. As a dispatcher for a freight service, you realize that there are 225 packages to be loaded onto trucks for Saturday delivery. An individual loader can load 25 packages onto a truck in an hour. How many loaders will you call in to get all packages loaded in one hour?

   A. 5

   B. 9

   C. 10

   D. 11

   E. 12

Account Balance Jan 1	$2,365.78
Purchase Jan 4	-123.67
Purchase Jan 12	- 345.79
Deposit Jan 17	276.77

5. As the driver of a refrigerated truck, you are concerned about your shipment. At the beginning of the route, the interior temperature was 28 °F. After making a few deliveries, the temperature had dropped to −4 °F. What was the change in temperature when you took the second measurement?

A. −32

B. −28

C. −4

D. 4

E. 32

6. Based on this account statement, what is the total change in the account due to the purchases on January 4 and January 12?

A. −$221.12

B. −$375.43

C. −$402.87

D. −$469.46

E. −$521.12

ANSWER KEY

Item 1: **C** 14 + 19 + 7 + 36 = 76

Item 2: **D** 13 × 35 = 455

Item 3: **C** 23 − 7 = 16

Item 4: **B** 225 ÷ 25 = 9

Item 5: **A** −4 − (−28) = −32

Item 6: **D** −123.67 + (−345.79) = −469.46

SKILL

2

Perform Basic
Arithmetic
Calculations
to Solve
Workplace
Problems

Apply
Computations
to Solve
Workplace
Problems

Solve
Measurement
Problems

Make Spending
Decisions
to Solve
Workplace
Problems

USE FRACTIONS, DECIMALS, AND PERCENTAGES TO SOLVE WORKPLACE PROBLEMS

In the transportation, distribution, and logistics industry, workers come across quantities represented in many different ways. A shipping clerk may need to calculate percentages to add shipping charges to a bill. The ability to perform workplace calculations using different forms of numbers is an important workplace skill.

1. In your job as a warehouse payroll clerk, you need to figure out what to pay each worker in one department that worked 80 hours of overtime last week. Ted worked 32 hours of the overtime. What percent of the overtime did he work?

    A. 4%

    B. 33%

    C. 36%

    D. 40%

    E. 50%

2. As a taxi driver, you charge a rate of $2.40 per mile. Your destination is $4\frac{1}{2}$ miles from your starting point. How much is the total fare?

    A. $6.90

    B. $7.87

    C. $8.33

    D. $10.80

    E. $18.10

3. As a port manager, you are trying to increase efficiency. Four ships are travelling to the same destination. Two ships are 0.5 full, one is 0.75 full, and one is only 0.25 full. If you consolidate the cargo, how many ships will you need?

    A. 1

    B. 1.5

    C. 2

    D. 3

    E. 3.5

4. As a package delivery person, you spend $3\frac{1}{2}$ hours delivering packages each day. Your work week is Monday through Friday. How many hours does it take to deliver packages in a week?

    A. 15

    B. $15\frac{1}{2}$

    C. $16\frac{1}{2}$

    D. 17

    E. $17\frac{1}{2}$

5. As a traffic safety consultant, your organization has received a grant for a safety belt program. Of the grant amount, $\frac{1}{6}$ is used for newspaper ads, $\frac{1}{3}$ for television ads, and $\frac{1}{3}$ for radio ads. What fraction of the grant money is used for advertising?

A. $\frac{1}{2}$

B. $\frac{2}{3}$

C. $\frac{4}{6}$

D. $\frac{3}{4}$

E. $\frac{5}{6}$

6. You load a beverage distribution truck so that $\frac{1}{5}$ of the load is regular cola, $\frac{2}{5}$ is diet cola, and $\frac{1}{5}$ is bottled water. What fraction represents how much of the truck has been loaded?

A. $\frac{11}{10}$

B. $\frac{3}{5}$

C. $\frac{11}{15}$

D. $\frac{4}{5}$

E. $\frac{5}{5}$

7. You work as a package handler for the food contractor that provides the space station's prepackaged meals. You will be packing some of the dehydrated drink mixes for the next supply delivery. You find that $\frac{2}{5}$ of the astronauts like hot coffee, $\frac{1}{5}$ like hot tea, and $\frac{1}{5}$ like hot cider for breakfast. What fraction of the beverages you pack constitute hot beverages?

A. $\frac{1}{4}$

B. $\frac{4}{15}$

C. $\frac{1}{2}$

D. $\frac{3}{4}$

E. $\frac{4}{5}$

8. As a sales manager, you have just signed a contract with a new customer who will purchase what comes out to 20 percent of your production capacity. Your sales reports indicate that current customers buy $\frac{3}{4}$ of your production capacity. You need to determine how the new contract will impact your inventory. Once the new contract takes effect, what percent of your production capacity remains unsold?

A. 5%

B. 7%

C. 10%

D. 12%

E. 15%

ANSWER KEY

Item 1: **D** $32 \div 80 = 0.4$; $0.4 \times 100 = 40\%$

Item 2: **D** $2.40 \times 4.5 = 10.80$

Item 3: **C** $0.5 + 0.5 + 0.75 + 0.25 = 2$

Item 4: **E** $3\frac{1}{2} = \frac{7}{2}$; $\frac{7}{2} \times 5 = \frac{35}{2} = 17\frac{1}{2}$

Item 5: **E** $\frac{1}{6} + \frac{2}{6} + \frac{2}{6} = \frac{5}{6}$

Item 6: **D** $\frac{1}{5} + \frac{2}{5} + \frac{1}{5} = \frac{4}{5}$

Item 7: **E** $\frac{2}{5} + \frac{1}{5} + \frac{1}{5} = \frac{4}{5}$

Item 8: **A** $3 \div 4 = 0.75$; $0.75 \times 100 = 75$; $75 + 20 = 95$; $100 - 95 = 5\%$

USE GENERAL PROBLEM SOLVING

Some mathematical calculations require more than one operation. A customs broker may need to use multiple calculations to track the duties and tariffs due on a shipment. Being able to quickly perform such calculations can improve a transportation, distribution, and logistics worker's efficiency.

1. During your workday as an airport shuttle driver, you make many trips to and from the terminal. On eleven trips, your bus is at capacity with 25 passengers. On the twelfth trip, you only had 13 passengers. How many passengers did you have in all?

   A.   49

   B.   275

   C.   288

   D.   375

   E.   600

2. You work as a packager at a shipping warehouse. You have used half of your boxes and decide to go get 16 more from the supply room. Now you have 38 boxes. How many boxes did you start with?

   A.   16

   B.   22

   C.   24

   D.   38

   E.   44

3. In your job as a route planner, you are responsible for planning the delivery routes for your company's drivers. You plan a route that initially covers 153 miles. However, one customer calls to cancel an order, which takes 17 miles off the route. You then receive a last-minute delivery, which puts another 24 miles on the driver's route. What is the length of the route now?

   A.   17 miles

   B.   24 miles

   C.   112 miles

   D.   136 miles

   E.   160 miles

4. In your job as a mechanic for a limousine company, you often have to purchase parts from the local auto supply store. You take $40 from the petty cash drawer and purchase four spark plugs. Each spark plug costs $5.99. How much change did you get back?

   A. $5.99

   B. $16.04

   C. $17.04

   D. $23.96

   E. $24.96

5. In your job as a livestock hauler, you earn $8 an hour for the first 40 hours you work in a week and $12 an hour for every hour after that. Each week you have $123 deducted from your check for income taxes and retirement. What is your take-home pay for a week in which you work 50 hours?

A. $317

B. $373

C. $440

D. $563

E. $813

6. As a warehouse manager, you supervise 98 workers. Of these, 10 receive a wage of $350 per day and the rest receive $255 per day. A week is equal to 6 working days. How much do you pay each week in wages?

A. $25,940

B. $43,440

C. $129,700

D. $138,140

E. $155,640

7. As the fleet manager for a taxi company, you track the maintenance for the cars. One car is due for an oil change. The mechanic purchases 5 quarts of oil at $8.49 per quart and an oil filter for $9.86. What is the total cost?

A. $23.35

B. $52.31

C. $57.79

D. $91.75

E. $133.01

8. You work as a park-and-ride bus driver for a large city. The city is trying to promote mass transit, and asks you to give 2 passes for free rides to every passenger. On your first run, you have 38 passengers. On your second run, you have 41 passengers. On your third and final run, you have 27 passengers. How many passes did you give out?

A. 108

B. 171

C. 174

D. 185

E. 212

ANSWER KEY

Item 1: **C** $11 \times 25 = 275$; $275 + 13 = 288$

Item 2: **E** $38 - 16 = 22$; $22 \times 2 = 44$

Item 3: **E** $153 - 17 = 136$; $136 + 24 = 160$

Item 4: **B** $5.99 \times 4 = 23.96$; $40.00 - 23.96 = \$16.04$

Item 5: **A** $40 \times 8 = 320$; $10 \times 12 = 120$; $320 + 120 - 123 = \$317$

Item 6: **E** $10 \times 350 = 3,500$; $(98 - 10) \times 255 = 22,440$; $3,500 + 22,440 = 25,940$; $25,940 \times 6 = \$155,640$

Item 7: **B** $5 \times 8.49 = 42.45$; $9.86 + 42.45 = \$52.31$

Item 8: **E** $38 + 41 + 27 = 106$; $106 \times 2 = 212$

SOLVE PROBLEMS IN GEOMETRY

Knowing how to determine the perimeters and areas of objects and spaces is an important skill in the transportation, distribution, and logistics industry. A storage manager may need to determine the area available in a warehouse to know how much inventory can be stored. At different times, the manager may need to calculate the perimeters or areas of a variety of shapes.

1. You are a mass transit engineer developing a new park-and-ride facility. To ensure the safety of the vehicles parked on your lot, you must purchase fencing for the perimeter of the square-shaped lot. One side of the square is 127.26 meters. What is the perimeter of this square?

   A. 254.52 meters

   B. 509.04 meters

   C. 1,272.60 meters

   D. 2,545.20 meters

   E. 5,090.40 meters

2. As a packaging supervisor, you need to determine the square footage of pallets that will be used for shipping. Each pallet is a rectangle measuring 4 feet by 3 feet. What is the area of a pallet?

   A. 7 square feet

   B. 12 square feet

   C. 14 square feet

   D. 24 square feet

   E. 48 square feet

3. Your job as a livestock hauler requires that you purchase a livestock trailer. The trailer is 32 feet long by 7 feet wide. What is the area of the trailer?

   A. 39 square feet

   B. 78 square feet

   C. 146 square feet

   D. 224 square feet

   E. 896 square feet

4. You are a warehouse manager planning for the resurfacing of the loading dock. The loading dock is triangular in shape with a base of 120 feet and a height of 180 feet. What is the area of the loading dock?

   A. 300 square feet

   B. 1,080 square feet

   C. 2,600 square feet

   D. 10,800 square feet

   E. 21,600 square feet

5. Your job as a transportation engineer's assistant has you examining bridges. To prevent concrete deterioration, columns supporting highways and bridges are to be coated with a polymer. You know that the diameter of most supporting columns is 6 feet. What is the circumference of the column?

   A. 9 feet

   B. 18.84 feet

   C. 20.46 feet

   D. 24.52 feet

   E. 25.12 feet

6. As a traffic engineer, you plan to incorporate a landscaped traffic circle at a new intersection. In order to not impede traffic, the diameter of the traffic circle can be no more than 250 feet. The construction company building the traffic circle charges for concrete by the square foot. What is the area of the traffic circle?

   A. 785 square feet

   B. 1,570 square feet

   C. 24,679 square feet

   D. 36,682 square feet

   E. 49,062.5 square feet

7. Part of your job as an industrial architect is to equip new warehouses with needed machines, tools, and other equipment. For a new warehouse, you determine that a conveyor belt 4 feet wide and 16 feet long is needed in order to fit the largest packages. Pricing of conveyor belts is stated in square feet. What is the area of this conveyor belt?

   A. 20 square feet

   B. 46 square feet

   C. 56 square feet

   D. 64 square feet

   E. 76 square feet

8. You are the assistant logistics manager for the distribution department of a large home improvement chain. Due to expansion, your company is considering buying an existing warehouse. If the warehouse is 200 feet by 520 feet, what is its area?

   A. 200 square feet

   B. 520 square feet

   C. 720 square feet

   D. 10,400 square feet

   E. 104,000 square feet

ANSWER KEY

Item 1: **B** 127.26 × 4 = 509.04 meters

Item 2: **B** 4 × 3 = 12 square feet

Item 3: **D** 32 × 7 = 224 square feet

Item 4: **D** 120 × 180 = 21,600; 21,600 ÷ 2 = 10,800 square feet

Item 5: **B** 6 × 3.14 = 18.84 feet

Item 6: **E** 250 ÷ 2 = 125; 125 × 125 × 3.14 = 49,062.5 square feet

Item 7: **D** 4 × 16 = 64 square feet

Item 8: **E** 200 × 520 = 104,000 square feet

CALCULATE WITH CONVERSIONS AND FORMULAS

Some calculations in transportation, distribution, and logistics may require using conversions and formulas. As a rail-track layer, you may need to calculate the length of track that has been laid based on different lengths of track that have been used. You may also need to convert minutes into hours to find out how long the job has taken.

1. You are a document delivery driver, and you bring a letter from a lawyer's office to the client's office. The client gives you six quarters, two dimes, and a penny for the balance due on her delivery. How much money did she give you?

   A. $1.21

   B. $1.46

   C. $1.61

   D. $1.71

   E. $1.75

2. As a shipping clerk, it takes you 240 minutes to enter shipping information into the computer for 48 packages. After completing this task, how many hours remain in your 8-hour shift?

   A. 1

   B. 2

   C. 3

   D. 4

   E. 5

3. The work day is over for you as a customer shipping clerk at the package delivery company, and you must total the amount of money in your cash register. You have three $20 bills, four $10 bills, two $5 bills, seven $1 bills, six quarters, eight dimes, six nickels, and eight pennies that need to be deposited. How much money is in your cash register at the end of your shift?

   A. $75.50

   B. $81.28

   C. $105.17

   D. $112.28

   E. $119.68

4. In your job as a commuter bus driver, you leave the park-and-ride facility at 6:30 a.m. Your first stop is $\frac{3}{4}$ of an hour later. The second stop is scheduled for 15 minutes after that. The final stop is 15 minutes later. At what time do you reach your final stop?

   A. 6:30 a.m.

   B. 6:45 a.m.

   C. 7:15 a.m.

   D. 7:30 a.m.

   E. 7:45 a.m.

5. You recently took a job as a commercial motor vehicle driver. According to federal Hours of Service rules, you have a limit of 14 hours of driving within a 24-hour period. Your log for the day shows that you have driven the following segments: 4 hours 15 minutes, 4 hours 15 minutes, and 4 hours 30 minutes. How many hours have you driven for the day?

    A. 12 hours 10 minutes

    B. 12 hours 45 minutes

    C. 13 hours

    D. 13 hours 10 minutes

    E. 14 hours

6. You are the assistant manager of a delivery service. Your boss has asked you to track the mileage of a new van that was purchased. The van has a 35-gallon gas tank, and the driver reports driving 560 miles on a tank of gas. What is the van's miles per gallon (mpg)?

    A. 0.0625 mpg

    B. 16 mpg

    C. 525 mpg

    D. 595 mpg

    E. 19,600 mpg

7. As a warehouse clerk, you make $10.00 per hour. You get 1.5 times your hourly rate for any hours over 40 that you work in a week. You worked 47 hours this week and 42 hours last week. How much money did you earn last week?

    A. $415

    B. $430

    C. $435

    D. $445

    E. $505

8. You are a airport shuttle dispatcher. Today, you worked from 6:30 a.m. until 11:45 a.m., took 45 minutes for a break, then worked 4 more hours. When did you return from your break?

    A. 7:15 a.m.

    B. 10:30 a.m.

    C. 12:30 p.m.

    D. 3:34 p.m.

    E. 4:30 p.m.

ANSWER KEY

Item 1: **D** $6 \times 0.25 = 1.50$; $2 \times 0.10 = 0.20$; $1.50 + 0.20 = 0.01 = \$1.71$

Item 2: **D** $240 \div 60 = 4$; $8 - 4 = 4$

Item 3: **E** $60 + 40 + 10 + 7 + 1.50 + 0.80 + 0.30 + 0.08 = \$119.68$

Item 4: **E** $60 \times \frac{3}{4} = 45$; $0{:}45 + 0{:}15 + 0{:}15 + 6{:}30 = 7{:}45$ a.m.

Item 5: **C** $4{:}15 + 4{:}15 + 4{:}30 = 13$ hours

Item 6: **B** $560 \div 35 = 16$ mpg

Item 7: **B** $40 \times 10 = 400$; $1.5 \times 2 \times 10 = 30$; $400 + 30 = \$430$

Item 8: **C** $11{:}45 + 0{:}45 = 12{:}30$

MANIPULATE FORMULAS TO SOLVE PROBLEMS

For some calculations in transportation, distribution, and logistics, a formula may need to be manipulated to solve a problem. For example, a logistics analyst may need to manipulate a formula to predict the true cost in time and personnel needed to ship a particular item. Workers should be able to work with formulas such as these to find the information required.

1. You are a manager for a delivery service. To protect your delivery vans when they are not in use, you would like to build a fence around the parking lot. You have purchased 432 feet of fencing, and the area you fence in will be a square. How long can each side of the fence be?

    A. 26 feet

    B. 54 feet

    C. 108 feet

    D. 144 feet

    E. 216 feet

2. As a packaging supervisor, you decide to install anti-fatigue flooring in the warehouse's packaging line. The packaging line is 42 feet long, and you have 210 square feet of flooring material. How wide will the anti-fatigue flooring be?

    A. 5 feet

    B. 10 feet

    C. 42 feet

    D. 126 feet

    E. 168 feet

3. As a livestock hauler, you must make sure that the trailer fits in the space allotted for loading and unloading livestock. The stockyards provide a space that is 7,200 square feet for your truck and trailer. A sign indicates that the space is 12 feet wide. How long is the space?

    A. 300 feet

    B. 600 feet

    C. 2,400 feet

    D. 1,800 feet

    E. 3,600 feet

4. You are a warehouse manager planning to add high-contrast paint along the perimeter of your loading dock to help prevent falls. The loading dock is a rectangle with a width of 135 feet. You paint a total of 560 feet. What is the length of the loading dock?

    A. 4 feet

    B. 135 feet

    C. 145 feet

    D. 270 feet

    E. 290 feet

5. As a shipping specialist, your customer asks for a mailing tube to ship some blueprints. You choose a mailing tube with a circumference of 15.7 inches. What is the diameter of the mailing tube?

   A. 2.24 inches

   B. 3.14 inches

   C. 5 inches

   D. 18.84 inches

   E. 49.298 inches

6. You work as a helicopter pilot. In order for you to land the helicopter on an office building's helipad, you must be sure that the length of the helicopter is shorter than the diameter of the landing area. The building manager informs you that the landing area's circumference is 78.5 feet. What is the diameter of the landing area?

   A. 3.14 feet

   B. 12.5 feet

   C. 18 feet

   D. 24.28 feet

   E. 25 feet

7. As a taxi driver, a passenger asks you to get to his destination in 15 minutes. The destination is 8 miles away. How many miles per hour would you need to travel to fulfill his request?

   A. 32 miles per hour

   B. 35 miles per hour

   C. 40 miles per hour

   D. 45 miles per hour

   E. 52 miles per hour

8. As a pilot for a shipping company, you often fly from Chicago to Atlanta. You travel at 284 miles per hour and fly 710 miles between the two cities. How long does the trip take?

   A. 1.5 hours

   B. 2 hours

   C. 2.5 hours

   D. 3 hours

   E. 3.5 hours

ANSWER KEY

Item 1: **C** 432 ÷ 4 = 108 feet

Item 2: **A** 210 ÷ 42 = 5 feet

Item 3: **B** 7,200 ÷ 12 = 600 feet

Item 4: **C** 560 − (2 × 135) = 290; 290 ÷ 2 = 145 feet

Item 5: **C** 15.7 ÷ 3.14 = 5 inches

Item 6: **E** 78.5 ÷ 3.14 = 25 feet

Item 7: **A** 8 ÷ 0.25 = 32 miles per hour

Item 8: **C** 710 ÷ 284 = 2.5 hours

CALCULATE COSTS AND DISCOUNTS

Some jobs in the transportation, distribution, and logistics industry require workers to calculate costs and discounts. A billing clerk, for instance, may need to calculate a discount for a purchaser shipping a big order of items to one location.

1. You are the fleet supervisor for a distribution company. You want to replace your diesel delivery vans with hybrid fuel delivery vans. Operation costs are $0.55 per mile for your current diesel delivery vans. You will save 20 percent per mile by switching to the hybrid van. What is the operation cost of the hybrid van?

   A. $0.11 per mile

   B. $0.20 per mile

   C. $0.38 per mile

   D. $0.44 per mile

   E. $0.53 per mile

2. As a document delivery driver, the price of gasoline directly impacts your profit. Gasoline averages $2.368 per gallon, but is expected to increase 18 percent next year. What will the average cost of gasoline be next year?

   A. $2.135

   B. $2.368

   C. $2.498

   D. $2.794

   E. $2.966

3. In your position as an inventory clerk for a beverage company, you notice that the bulk cost of a coffee drink increased from $500 to $800. What is the percentage increase in the bulk cost of the coffee drink?

   A. 30%

   B. 35%

   C. 37.5%

   D. 60%

   E. 62.5%

4. A local export company has hired you as a purchaser. Company A offers a shipping container measuring 2,750 cubic feet at $6.50 per cubic foot. Company B offers the same size container for 25% less. How much money will you save if you use Company B?

   A. $3,010.25

   B. $4,468.75

   C. $5,585.50

   D. $13,406.25

   E. $17,875

5. As a conveyor operator, you made $30,350 last year. You will receive a 0.7 percent increase in salary this year. What will your salary for this year be?

   A. $30,562.45

   B. $32,474.50

   C. $34,745

   D. $51,595

   E. $212,450

6. You are the import supervisor for a grocery chain. You want to purchase grapes from a vendor at a cost of $20 per box. In the time you are deciding, the price of grapes increases by 7 percent. What would the new price of a box of grapes be?

   A. $20.07

   B. $20.70

   C. $21.07

   D. $21.14

   E. $21.40

7. As fleet manager for an airline, you are responsible for purchasing jet fuel. The excise tax for jet fuel is 21.8 cents per gallon. It is being increased by 65 percent. What will the new excise tax per gallon be?

   A. 7.63 cents

   B. 13.52 cents

   C. 29.43 cents

   D. 35.97 cents

   E. 36.40 cents

8. You work for an airline as a reservation agent. Last year, the price for airline tickets dropped 10.9 percent to an average price of $310. What was the price before the drop?

   A. $311.09

   B. $320.90

   C. $347.92

   D. $419.00

   E. $647.90

ANSWER KEY

Item 1: **D** $0.55 \times 0.8 = \$0.44$ per mile

Item 2: **D** $2.368 + (2.368 \times 0.18) = 2.794$

Item 3: **D** $800 - 500 = 300; 300 \div 500 = 0.600; 0.600 \times 100 = 60.0$

Item 4: **B** $25\% = 0.25; 6.5 \times 2,750 = 17,875; 17,875 \times 0.25 = \$4,468.75$

Item 5: **A** $0.007 \times 30,350 = 212.45; 30,350 + 212.45 = \$30,562.45$

Item 6: **E** $0.07 \times 20 = 1.40; 20 + 1.40 = \$21.40$

Item 7: **D** $0.218 \times 0.65 = 0.1417; 0.218 + 0.1417 = \$0.3597 = 35.97$ cents

Item 8: **C** $100\% - 10.9\% = 89.1\%; 310 \div 0.891 = \$347.92$

MAKE CONSUMER COMPARISONS

Transportation, distribution, and logistics workers who make purchasing decisions or recommendations must often make calculations that compare two or more purchasing options. A logistics engineer may compare shipping bids and use that information to complete an estimate of the total cost of a project. Being able to make these calculations and find the best deal is an important industry skill.

1. You manage a fleet of cars for a limousine service. One of your cars needs a thorough cleaning. Company A charges a flat detailing fee of $430. Company B charges $65 per hour plus $90 for supplies. The work takes 5.5 hours. If you chose Company A, how much money would you save?

   A. $17.50

   B. $65

   C. $292.50

   D. $382.50

   E. $430

2. You work as a cross-country delivery driver. You will need to stay in a motel for 6 nights on your upcoming trip. Doing an Internet search, you find that you can get a rate of $78 per night at Motel A and $85 per night at Motel B. How much will you save on a 6-night stay at Motel A?

   A. $25

   B. $37

   C. $42

   D. $45

   E. $50

3. As a transportation manager, you are always looking for ways to save your company money. A supplier came to you recently and gave you prices on motor oil. He said he can sell you oil in 5-quart containers at $5.80 per container or he can provide 2-quart containers at $2.30 per quart. If you buy containers with a lower price per unit, how much will you pay per quart?

   A. $0.95

   B. $1.01

   C. $1.09

   D. $1.15

   E. $1.16

4. As a buyer for a grocery warehouse, you need to purchase 80 pounds of grapes. One vendor offers grapes for $2.23 per pound. Another vendor sells 8-pound crates of grapes for $17.20. If you choose the cheaper vendor, how much will you save when buying 80 pounds of grapes?

   A. $0.08

   B. $0.64

   C. $0.80

   D. $2.15

   E. $6.40

5. In your position as fleet manager for a company, you are responsible for getting company cars for the best possible price. One dealership offers you sedans at $32,500 each. Another dealership offers you a fleet of six of the same sedan for $190,000. If you need six cars, which is the better option, and how much will you save?

   A. Buying the cars individually saves $2,500.

   B. Buying the fleet of six cars saves $2,500.

   C. Buying the cars individually saves $5,000.

   D. Buying the fleet of six cars saves $5,000.

   E. The price is the same regardless of which dealership you buy from.

6. As a scheduler for a long-distance moving company, you are trying to reduce costs for employees who travel overnight. Motel A has offered a rate of $84 per night including breakfast. Motel B has offered $78 per night for the room and $3.50 for a hot breakfast. You know you must book 120 nights for the year. Which motel provides more savings for the 120 nights, and how much will you save?

   A. Motel B saves $250.

   B. Motel B saves $300.

   C. Motel A saves $780.

   D. Motel A saves $815.

   E. The cost is the same.

7. As a warehouse manager, you are replacing a conveyor belt. Business A charges $1,500 including labor, but it offers you a 15% new customer discount. Business B charges $1,200 plus $125 labor. Business C charges $1,675 total, but you have a credit with Business C for $219. What is the lowest cost you can pay for the belt?

   A. $1,219

   B. $1225

   C. $1,275

   D. $1,325

   E. $1,456

8. As a warehouse manager, you need to replace the flooring on the loading dock. The rectangular dock is 28 feet by 40 feet. You have three bids for the job. Bid A is $5.75 per square foot plus $150 labor. Bid B is $5.95 total per square foot. Bid C is $6,980 total, with 5% off for a new customer. What is the least you can pay for this job?

   A. $6,440

   B. $6,590

   C. $6,631

   D. $6,664

   E. $6,980

ANSWER KEY

Item 1: **A** $65 \times 5.5 = 357.50$; $357.50 + 90.00 = 447.50$; $447.50 - 430.00 = \$17.50$

Item 2: **C** $78 \times 6 = 468$; $85 \times 6 = 510$; $510 - 468 = \$42$

Item 3: **D** $5.80 \div 5 = 1.16$; $2.30 \div 2 = \$1.15$

Item 4: **E** $17.20 \div 8 = 2.15$; $2.23 - 2.15 = 0.08$; $80 \times 0.08 = \$6.40$

Item 5: **D** $6 \times 32,500 = 195,000$; $195,000 - 190,000 = \$5,000$

Item 6: **B** $78.00 + 3.50 = 81.50$; $84 - 81.50 = 2.50$; $2.50 \times 120 = \$300$

Item 7: **C** Company A: $1,500 \times 0.15 = 225$; $1,500 - 225 = \$1,275$;
Company B: $1,200 + 125 = \$1,325$; Company C: $1,675 - 219 = \$1,456$

Item 8: **B** Area $= 28 \times 40 = 1,120$ square feet; Bid A: $5.75 \times 1,120 = 6,440$; $6,440 + 150 = \$6,590$;
Bid B: $5.95 \times 1,120 = \$6,664$; Bid C: $6,980 \times 0.05 = 349$; $6,980 - 349 = \$6,631$

CAREER CLUSTERS AND PATHWAYS

A career cluster is a grouping of jobs and industries based on common characteristics. A career pathway is an area of focus within a career cluster. You can explore each of the following career clusters and pathways in McGraw-Hill Workforce's *Career Companion* series.

Agriculture, Food & Natural Resources
Food Products and Processing Systems
Plant Systems
Animal Systems
Power, Structural & Technical Systems
Natural Resources Systems
Environmental Service Systems
Agribusiness Systems

Architecture & Construction
Design/Pre-Construction
Construction
Maintenance/Operations

Arts, Audio/Video Technology & Communications
Audio and Video Technology and Film
Printing Technology
Visual Arts
Performing Arts
Journalism and Broadcasting
Telecommunications

Business Management & Administration
General Management
Business Information Management
Human Resources Management
Operations Management
Administrative Support

Education & Training
Administration and Administrative Support
Professional Support Services
Teaching/Training

Finance
Securities & Investments
Business Finance
Accounting
Insurance
Banking Services

Government & Public Administration
Governance
National Security
Foreign Service
Planning
Revenue and Taxation
Regulation
Public Management and Administration

Health Science
Therapeutic Services
Diagnostic Services
Health Informatics
Support Services
Biotechnology Research and Development

Hospitality & Tourism
Restaurants and Food/Beverage Services
Lodging
Travel & Tourism
Recreation, Amusements & Attractions

Human Services
Early Childhood Development & Services
Counseling & Mental Health Services
Family & Community Services
Personal Care Services
Consumer Services

Information Technology
Network Systems
Information Support and Services
Web and Digital Communications
Programming and Software Development

Law, Public Safety, Corrections & Security
Correction Services
Emergency and Fire Management Services
Security & Protective Services
Law Enforcement Services
Legal Services

Manufacturing
Production
Manufacturing Production Process Development
Maintenance, Installation & Repair
Quality Assurance
Logistics & Inventory Control
Health, Safety and Environmental Assurance

Marketing
Marketing Management
Professional Sales
Merchandising
Marketing Communications
Marketing Research

Science, Technology, Engineering & Mathematics
Engineering and Technology
Science and Math

Transportation, Distribution & Logistics
Transportation Operations
Logistics Planning and Management Services
Warehousing and Distribution Center Operations
Facility and Mobile Equipment Maintenance
Transportation Systems/Infrastructure Planning, Management and Regulation
Health, Safety and Environmental Management
Sales and Service